MINISTRY AND AUTHORITY IN THE CATHOLIC CHURCH

MINISTRY AND AUTHORITY IN THE CATHOLIC CHURCH

===

Edmund Hill, OP

GEOFFREY CHAPMAN
LONDON

A Geoffrey Chapman book published by
Cassell Publishers Limited
Artillery House, Artillery Row
London SW1P 1RT

First published 1988

ISBN 0 225 66527 1

British Library Cataloguing in Publication Data
Hill, Edmund
   Ministry and authority in the Catholic Church.
   1. Catholic Church. Authority
   I. Title
   262'.8

Typesetting by Fakenham Photosetting Ltd

Printed in Great Britain by Biddles Ltd, Guildford

CONTENTS

PREFACE

I wish to warn the reader from the beginning that this book is a work of advocacy, not of judicial impartiality. In it I am advocating one view, one theology of authority and ministry in the Church and attacking another. I am pleading a cause, I am taking a side, before the tribunal of Catholic public opinion. If anyone in response should decide to appear for the other side, criticise the theology I advocate and defend the other, I would be delighted. I am continually disappointed in my efforts to provoke the other party (whom in this book I call magisterial papalists, or MPs for short) into debate, by such means as occasional letters to *The Tablet*.

The other party, being actually in control, and authoritarian in temperament, and regarding its own rightness as axiomatic, adopts a technique in the face of criticism that one is familiar with from the practice of authoritarian secular régimes, like the South African government, for example. The first reaction is to ignore the criticism, not to hear it, to turn a deaf ear—the proverbial expression indicates that the technique is as old as sin itself. The next step, when it is no longer possible to pretend that the criticism is not there, is to evade it by attributing all kinds of dubious motives to the critics, from mere crankiness to malice. The actual criticisms levelled are hardly ever met objectively for what they are, and either answered or accepted.

Here then I am challenging the authorities in the Church, those who support the magisterial papalist line, to do just that; and I am inviting my readers to acknowledge, and to ask their spiritual fathers in God to acknowledge, that I have at least made out a case which ought to be answered.

To the innocent child in the story
who asked
why the Emperor had no clothes

ABBREVIATIONS

AS   *Acta Synodalia Sacrosancti Concilii Oecumenici Vaticani* II

Dz   *Enchiridion Symbolorum*, ed. H. Denzinger, rev. A.
      Schönmetzer, 33rd edition, 1965

MC   Ministerial collegialist

MP   Magisterial papalist

PG   *Patrologiae Cursus Completus, Series Graeca*,
      ed. J.-P. Migne

PL   *Patrologiae Cursus Completus, Series Latina*,
      ed. J.-P. Migne

TWO CATHOLIC OPINIONS ON AUTHORITY IN THE CHURCH

It is commonly assumed by ordinary Catholics that there is only one Catholic view of authority in the Church, the one that is taken for granted and put into practice by the Vatican. This view is assumed to be Catholic doctrine. Thus in a letter to *The Tablet*, 6 December 1986, a correspondent wrote:

> How can Fr Curran say in all honesty as a Catholic . . . that no one has a monopoly of the Holy Spirit? Is not that exactly what Jesus gave Peter when he said: 'I give you the keys of my Church. What you bind on earth shall be bound in heaven, and what you loose on earth shall be loosed in heaven'? How else can that be interpreted other than that the Pope—and his successors in perpetuity, given that Jesus did not intend to found a Church just for the duration of Peter's life—was given a monopoly of the Holy Spirit?

These are not, of course, the words of a Vatican theologian, but they illustrate how Vatican theology is readily assumed by the ordinary pious Catholic to be Catholic doctrine. The correspondent does not understand how Fr Curran can disagree with his own exaggeration of this theology 'as a Catholic'.

But the truth is that within the bounds of Catholic orthodoxy it is possible to hold other views about authority and ministry in the Catholic Church, which differ widely from those of the dominant theology that at present governs the practice of the Roman Curia. My purpose in this book will be to criticise relentlessly this dominant theology of authority, and to propose another which, I will suggest, is more faithful to the gospel, to the most authentic Catholic tradition and—most immediately—to the spirit of Vatican II.

Vatican II unequivocally committed the whole Catholic Church to the ecumenical movement, that is to working for the unity of all Christians; and equally unequivocally it acknowledged that this work is quite distinct from working for the conversion or reconciliation of individuals or groups to the Catholic Church. The Council also endorsed the principle of collegiality, which speaking roughly means 'power sharing', or shared authority. And Cardinal Wojtyła, in his speech accepting election as Pope John Paul II, said that the promotion of ecumenism and collegiality would be the chief aims of his policy as pope.

But the view of authority in the Church which is still dominant in the Vatican, and which the pope, to judge by any number of his actions and statements, seems to share, is simply not compatible either with ecumenism or with collegiality. It is, practically speaking, anti-ecumenical and anti-collegial.

To give one instance: on 24 November 1986 the BBC reported the pope as saying in New Zealand that the Roman Catholic Church cannot compromise its principles, and that its commitment to the ecumenical movement faced the other Christian Churches with new demands. To be sure, what the pope says and what the BBC reports him as saying are not necessarily quite the same thing. But what he is reported as saying is what he is heard by the world as saying. Now since the question of authority in the Church is generally acknowledged to be perhaps the most intractable obstacle to ecumenical progress, it may be assumed that the Roman idea of authority was at least one of the principles the pope had in mind. And taking his statement as reported, one can only say that it constituted a body blow to ecumenism. It was, in the strictest meaning of the word, scandalous. That is to say, it will have alienated Protestants and seriously discouraged Catholics from pursuing the ecumenical way—which has never, in any case, been a way of requiring any party to compromise its principles, but only to re-examine them critically and in the light of Christ. But the pope's statement as reported is redolent of the view of authority that prevails in the Vatican: namely that authority in the Catholic Church (to all intents and purposes papal authority) is in the last resort not to be questioned, beyond any human critical judgement, subject to divine judgement alone.

A. The two opinions

Let me now label and describe the two views of authority in the

Catholic Church which I shall be opposing to each other in the course of this book. I call the first view, the one at present in control of the levers of ecclesiastical power, *magisterial papalist*. It has a long history behind it. In the nineteenth and twentieth centuries it has been called 'ultramontane', the view of authority and the Church held 'beyond the mountains', i.e. south of the Alps, i.e. in Rome itself. Mediaeval historians call it, as it was expressed in the Middle Ages, simply 'papalist'. I call it 'magisterial papalist' because one of the most frequently employed terms in its armoury is *magisterium*, and because I wish to avoid any suggestion that its Catholic critics reject or deny the papal authority. As Catholics, committed to upholding the papacy and its authority as defined at Vatican I in 1870, we are all papalists.[1] But we are *not*, as Catholics, definitely not, committed to the ultramontane view of the papacy so succinctly reduced *ad absurdum* in the letter quoted above, which I therefore style magisterial papalist—MP for short.

The contrary view I shall be proposing I label *ministerial collegialist*—MC for short. It too has a long history behind it, and has taken many forms, not all of which by any means would I regard as acceptable. From the fifteenth to the nineteenth centuries it was most commonly known as Gallicanism—a view of the Church insisted on above all by the absolute monarchs of France before the French Revolution. From about 1800 onwards some British Catholics adopted the name 'cisalpine', meaning 'this side of the Alps' in contradistinction to 'ultramontane', beyond them. As it found expression in the Middle Ages it is called conciliarism by the historians—the movement that saw in general councils the only remedy for the ills of the Church when the papacy seemed, and was, morally bankrupt.

B. The magisterial papalist view

The MP theory of authority starts with Christ bestowing authority on Peter and the apostles, and only on Peter and the apostles. From them it passes to the pope and the bishops, and only to the pope and the bishops. They are the sole possessors of Christ-given authority in the Church.

1. Concentration of authority in the papacy

But in fact, in this view, this authority is really concentrated in the papacy. The pope, and he alone, enjoys the *plenitudo potestatis*, the fullness of authority. Only the more extreme, or less sophisticated, MPs maintain in theory that the bishops derive their authority immediately from the pope and not immediately from Christ, so that in the government of their dioceses they are no more than the pope's agents, representatives or lieutenants. Only two or three years ago I heard an excellent and senior priest refer to the Archbishop of Maseru, presiding at a function in his own archdiocese, as 'the Holy Father's representative'.

This, though clean contrary to the most formal statements of Vatican II,[2] is very understandable, because in practice all MPs envisage the government of the Church in this way, and the Vatican acts in this way. The Church is governed by the pope from Rome, with the assistance of his *curia* or court, in which he appoints all the bishops (with the rarest of exceptions), and from which he sends them directives and instructions all round the world. The pope with his fullness of authority is responsible, i.e. answerable, to no other human person or authority, but only to God. He is indeed an absolute monarch—and one can see that the papacy has for centuries been taking on the trappings of absolute monarchy, derived in the first place from the archetype of European absolute monarchies, the late Roman or Byzantine Empire. Thus he officially resides in a 'Sacred Palace'; his court is divided into 'Sacred Congregations'; he is assisted by 'the Sacred College of Cardinals'; he is 'the most holy Lord', 'the Holy Father'; he was until recently crowned with a triple tiara. And more down to earth, he appoints, as we observed, nearly all the bishops. Only in the present pontificate (and the brief one of John Paul I) have some of these trappings, but none of the substance, of absolute monarchy been laid aside.

2. *Magisterium* and hierarchy

Two further words are associated with this concept of authority in the Church: 'hierarchy' and '*magisterium*'. The pope and the bishops, to whom alone authority in the Church belongs, are in common ecclesiastical parlance known as 'the hierarchy'. It is an axiom of the MP party that our Lord instituted the Church as a 'hierarchical society'—in contrast, for example, to an egalitarian or democratic society; more precisely, as a society to be governed by hierarchs or high priests.

The authority of these hierarchs, pope and bishops, vests them with a power not only to govern but to *teach*—a *magisterium*, the authority of the *magister* or master in the sense of 'teacher'. The word '*magisterium*' in recent ecclesiastical documents (it is, theologically, a very recent word) is often concretised to mean those who exercise it, and sometimes qualified characteristically with the word 'sacred', so that you may come across such a phrase as 'It is the common teaching of the Sacred *Magisterium* that . . .' The reference, as often as not, will be simply to the pope or the Holy See.

3. Sacerdotalism, clericalism

Two other concepts colour the MP view of authority in the Church. We have observed the frequent use of the word 'sacred' in MP language. The usage derives, as I suggested, from Byzantium, not from Galilee. But its justification has come to be that the authority in question is essentially priestly or sacerdotal, and priests are by definition persons invested with sacred powers, and indeed are as such sacred persons. Now again in common Catholic parlance it is not only—or mainly—popes and bishops who are called priests, but ordinary Catholic clergymen like the author, collectively known as 'the clergy'. Technically we belong to the second rank of the hierarchy (in a slightly different sense now) of bishops, priests and deacons. So we are not, in theory, vested with any authority except what is delegated to us by bishops or pope. But again in practice we are commonly regarded by the faithful as vested with a kind of sacred authority, within very definite limits.[3]

So authority in the MP view is sacerdotal and hence clerical, because all priests belong to a class or caste called 'the clergy', from which of course all bishops and popes are drawn. And one of the chief concerns of the MP party is to preserve the sacredness— i.e. the distinctness or apartness in the service of God—of the clergy. Hence the absolute insistence on compulsory celibacy for the clergy, and the refusal even to discuss the matter, or related matters like the ordination of women.

The title of this book includes the word 'ministry', and the reader may have noticed that I have not used it at all in my description of the MP position. This is not because it does not occur in the MP vocabulary, but because when it is used in its strong sense as service of God and the community by persons in authority as servants, it is treated purely as a kind of moral ideal for such persons, who ought to regard their exercise of authority in that light—as I am sure very many of them do. But the concept of ministry or service is not seen in the MP scheme of things as *essentially* qualifying the notion of authority, which is defined without reference to it.

C. The ministerial collegialist view

I come now to the ministerial collegialist view, that is to the particular form of it which I prefer. There are various forms of it, no doubt, but here I can only state my own personal view.

To start again then with Christ, to whom 'all authority in heaven and on earth has been given' (Mt 28:18). MCs of my sort agree that he gave his authority to Peter and the apostles, and hence to the pope and the bishops as their heirs. But first of all we do not agree that the apostles derived their authority from or through Peter, and therefore we do not admit that bishops derive their authority from the pope. They are indeed subordinate to the pope in their exercise of their authority, but not merely his agents or delegates. They have—or should have by rights—their proper autonomy.

And secondly as an MC I hold that Christ did not share his authority *only* with Peter and the apostles, the pope and the bishops. I maintain that he also shared it with the whole Church, with *all* the faithful. When MPs assert that authority and *magisterium* are the prerogative exclusively of the hierarchy, they are ignoring certain important New Testament texts and misconstruing others, e.g. Jn 1:12; Gal 4:4–7; 1 Pet 2:5, 9; Rev 1:6; Mt 18:15–18.

1. 'Churches' and 'Church'

So as an MC I strongly disapprove of the concentration of all authority in the Holy See—or should I rather say that I see it as a purely historical development, something unknown in the first thousand years of Christian history; something that may possibly have had some value in the political contexts of mediaeval and post-Tridentine western Europe, but is now unrealistic and counter-productive.

I prefer to think of the Church, in fact, as a Church of Churches, not as one uniform society divided into administrative units called dioceses (another term borrowed from the administration of the late Roman Empire). Rather it is seen as a great number of local communities or Churches of believers (this is Paul's customary language—the Church of Corinth, the Church of Philippi, the Churches of Judaea etc.) united in their common faith and hope under the presiding charity of the local Church of Rome.[4] In the New Testament, when the universal Church is mentioned, which is rarely, it is not some world-wide organisation that is being referred to, with its administrative structure, but a heavenly or cosmic mystery or idea, which is embodied in each local Catholic Church, not constituted by them as by its parts.

Now there is no going back on the fact that the Church has become a world-wide organised society. But we MCs maintain that it really requires little or no central *government*, that its most natural form of organisation is on a regional basis in what used to be known as provincial councils or synods, presided over by metropolitans or primates (whose authority varied enormously from one region and period to another), and what are now known as bishops' conferences.

2. Churches as brotherhoods

Instead of thinking of the Church as essentially a hierarchical society, MCs consider the local Churches to be essentially brotherhoods—and the essence of the fraternal relationship is equality. They are, we agree, organised brotherhoods, with gradations of authority. But these are purely functional— necessary, yes, but not of the essence of the society. We are chary of the words 'hierarchy' and '*magisterium*', for reasons that will appear in later chapters. We cannot seriously consider teaching, or teaching authority, to be the exclusive concern of the hierarchy; a vast array of Christians, from parents and school teachers and catechists to parish priests, seminary professors and theologians, lay as well as clerical, are involved in handing on the true faith with a measure of authority, in maintaining and developing the tradition. Some of them are formally recognised as Doctors (i.e. teachers) and Fathers of the Church.

Nor is teaching the simple business of an active teacher handing on the goods to a passive audience, as much of the official use of the *magisterium* concept seems to imply. MCs simply reject the old distinction between *ecclesia docens* and *ecclesia discens*, the teaching and the learning Church, in so far as it was intended to refer to two groups of people, the hierarchy and the rest. The whole

Church in all its members from the pope down is both teaching and learning. The two processes are in fact practically identical. Teaching involves, means, implies, arguing, questioning, disagreeing, criticising, being convinced, being criticised, learning.

3. Authority as service

Finally MCs place great stress, in fact the main stress, on authority as service or ministry. We don't simply see this, like MPs, as a moral ideal to be set before persons in authoriy. To safeguard this essentially Christian quality of authority, we think it needs to be institutionalised, i.e. to be expressed in certain kinds of institution with which we are in fact quite familiar.

For instance, employers like to be able to choose their servants, though I admit this is not always possible. Well, members of Christian brotherhoods which we call local Churches should be able to choose their servants, namely their bishops and clergy, and not just have them appointed over them from above. This was indeed the ancient and canonical procedure; bishops were supposed to be elected by clergy and people.[5] All sorts of difficulties arose, to be sure. But I really do not see why, if Anglicans in most of the provinces of the Anglican communion can elect their bishops, not to mention the forms of election employed by Presbyterians and Congregationalists, it should be impossible for Roman Catholics to do it too.

And then law-making. We are familiar with representative institutions. So was the Catholic Church in bygone days, and indeed the old canon law, with its principle of 'what touches all should be approved by all' (*quod omnes tangit ab omnibus approbetur*), was a prime agent in the development of such institutions in mediaeval Europe. They serve to ensure, to some extent, that those in high authority act as the servants of the community they are meant to be. The idea that the pope is the sole legislator for the whole Church, and under him bishops are sole legislators for their dioceses, is a principle of absolute monarchies—'what seems good to the prince has the force of law' (*quod principi placuit legis habet vigorem*)—Byzantine, not evangelical.

In the following chapters I hope to provide the evidence to support my rejection of magisterial papalism and my championing of ministerial collegialism. The evidence will be taken from the New Testament, from Church history, and from an assessment of the most recent Councils, Vatican I and Vatican II.

NOTES

1 There are some exceptions, the best known, no doubt, being Hans Küng. But there are other Catholic theologians who do not think that Catholics are irrevocably committed to the definitions of 1870. Luis M. Bermejo, a Spanish Jesuit who has worked all his life in India, and writes in English, argues that it is by no means certain that we have to, or should treat the first Vatican Council—or any general council of the past millennium whose membership has been confined to the Latin Church—as in the strictest sense ecumenical. If it was not ecumenical, it could not make infallible definitions of doctrine; therefore its definition of papal primacy and infallibility was not itself infallible.

As the title of Fr Bermejo's book shows—*Towards Christian Reunion* (Gujarat Sahitya Prakash Anand, India)—the context of his argument is ecumenical discussion. What he is arguing towards is the assertion that the Roman Catholic Church, without necessarily giving up the papal doctrines defined at Vatican I (and reaffirmed almost obsessively at Vatican II), should not by rights make their acceptance by other Christian communions a *sine qua non* for reunion.

In the long run this may be so—who can tell? But in the short run I personally think his approach is a tactical mistake in the campaign within the Catholic Church to dislodge or outflank the ultramontane obstacle to ecumenical progress.

2 'Bishops govern the particular churches entrusted to them as the vicars and ambassadors of Christ . . . This power, which they personally exercise in Christ's name is proper, ordinary and immediate, although its exercise is ultimately regulated by the supreme authority of the Church . . . The pastoral office or the habitual and daily care of their sheep is entrusted to them completely. Nor are they to be regarded as vicars of the Roman Pontiff, for they exercise an authority which is proper to them . . .' (*Lumen Gentium*, 27: as in *The Documents of Vatican II*, ed. Walter J. Abbott, SJ, pp. 49–50).

3 If a priest, whether a theologian or not, says anything that seems novel, i.e. is not obviously related to what has been learned in catechism or heard regularly in Church, then a mental safety curtain will come down in the minds of many Catholics, and what he says will either not be heard, or ignored, or misrepresented or in the last resort rejected. The same is, I must concede, probably true if it is a bishop, cardinal or even a pope saying something that sounds novel. Fundamentally, this is as it should be. In the long run it is the *sensus fidelium* working, a contribution to that infallibility in believing which the whole People of God enjoys as its share in Christ's prophetic office (*Lumen Gentium*, 12). But in the short run it means that there is a built-in bias in the popular Catholic mind in favour of a naïve ultramontanism, as the letter quoted at the beginning of this chapter indicates. However, the widespread non-acceptance of some

of the teaching of Paul VI's encyclical *Humanae Vitae* by millions of ordinary Catholics shows that the ultramontane stronghold in the minds of 'simple Catholics' is by no means impregnable.

4 Cf. a phrase of St Ignatius of Antioch in his letter to the Christians of Rome, written as he was on his way to martyrdom in the Colosseum there about AD 110. Two things are remarkable about this letter, with respect to our present concern: first, the exceptional respect he shows to the Church of Rome, in comparison with all the other local Churches to which he wrote; secondly, that he never once mentions the bishop of the Roman Church, whereas reverence for the bishop was a major theme of all his letters to the other Churches. One plausible inference that can be drawn from this silence is that the Roman Church—conservative from the beginning—had not yet adopted the institution of episcopacy!

5 In the history of the Church there has been almost endless variety in the way in which bishops have been chosen. That the popular element in their election was still a reality in the fourth century, after the peace of Constantine, is shown by the two famous cases of St Ambrose in Milan and St Augustine in Hippo. But this element was difficult, indeed almost impossible to regulate canonically, and was occasionally riotous and violent. In the Middle Ages the canonical right of election belonged to cathedral chapters, but was more often than not overruled, or at least 'directed', by lay rulers. To counteract this lay control the popes first challenged the greater rulers, especially the German emperors, in what are known as the wars of investiture; and then from the thirteenth century on began extending the practice of what was known as papal 'provision' to bishoprics—and to other ecclesiastical offices. This in turn was resisted by lay rulers, notably by the kings of England, and by the fifteenth century it had become a matter of bargaining between the Holy See and the courts of Europe. Canonically speaking, papal provision to bishoprics was the exception right up to the promulgation of the Code of Canon Law in 1917. So its treatment as the norm in the New Code recently promulgated can hardly be regarded as an ancient tradition in the Catholic Church. Vestiges of the election by the people can be found in the current rite of ordination of a bishop, though it is now reduced to a token 'Thanks be to God' after the reading of the apostolic letter of mandate from the Holy See; however, the rubrics do admit '. . . or (the people) give their assent to the choice in some other way, according to local custom'.

2

AUTHORITY IN
THE NEW TESTAMENT

In this chapter I shall be examining, first, the nature of authority as redefined by Jesus in the gospels; second, the distribution of authority within the community of believers; and third, the various ways in which authority was deployed or exercised in the different local Churches of which we have evidence in the New Testament. We are, of course, only interested in authority as belonging to God and Jesus Christ, and as vested by Christ in his followers. We shall not take much notice of what the New Testament has to say—it is merely descriptive in any case—about the secular authority of such persons as Herod, or Caesar or Pilate, or even Satan, whose authority (and it is real enough) can I suppose be rightly called secular.

A. The nature of authority

1. Authority as ministry

I have just talked of Jesus redefining authority. He did it with one of his characteristically outrageous paradoxes by declaring that within the kingdom, within the brotherhood of his followers, all authority is ministerial. Before we look at the texts, let us just reflect for a moment how absurdly paradoxical the concept of ministerial authority really is. Authority ordinarily means the power to give commands and to enforce them; to lay down the law with little expectation of being gainsaid; to wield influence, to control, to rule, to guide effectively. Ministry, if we stick to the real meaning of the word, which is perhaps still more evident in the Greek equivalent *diakonia*, means simply to serve. In fact it means the opposite of authority; it means carrying out commands, accepting law as laid down by others, being ruled, controlled, influenced, or at most being an instrument through

which the possessor of authority exercises influence, control and
rule.

So 'ministerial authority' looks like a contradiction in terms. If
it is not to be that, then it has to involve either a radical, revolu-
tionary recasting of the idea of authority, or an evaporation of the
idea of ministry, of service. There can be no doubt which of the
two is involved when Jesus combines the two terms, not only in
the gospel texts but in his own person. There we see that the
notion of authority is radically recast, while the idea of service is
rigorously maintained in all its crude literalness. The authority of
Christ himself, and therefore of all who share in it, is an authority
only for the sake of service; an authority to wash the feet of the
disciples; an authority to care for others, to consider their interests; an authority to give his life as a ransom for many.

But let us look at the texts which merit scrutiny in some detail.

a. Mark 10:42–45
(and parallel, Matthew 20:25–28)

The context is the request of James and John for the highest places
in the kingdom, and the very natural indignation of 'the ten' at
this staggering presumption:

> And Jesus called them to him and said to them, 'You know
> that those who are supposed to rule over the Gentiles lord it
> over them, and their great men exercise authority over
> them. But it shall not be so among you; but whoever would
> be great among you must be your servant (Latin, *minister*),
> and whoever would be first among you must be slave of all.
> For the Son of man also came not to be served but to serve,
> and to give his life as a ransom for many'.

Notice how he first gives the vulgar secular view of authority:
rulers or chiefs are expected to lord it over people, their authority
is one of domination (the Latin word here), and exercising authority (very much from above, according to the untranslatable
nuance of the Greek *katexousiazousin*) is something that naturally
belongs to the great—the phrase would be more accurately translated 'it is their great men who exercise authority over them'.

And then the thunderous contrast: 'It shall not be so among
you'. Among you greatness will be different, and primacy or
being first will be different; among you these titles to honour and
precedence will be a matter of being servants and slaves: of being
ministers, not *magisters*; of ministry, not *magisterium*.

b. *Matthew 23:8–12*

The term *magisterium* is not used in the Marcan text above. But it is found in a text from Matthew 23 which provides what we may call the sociological context in which Jesus redefines authority (or simply replaces it by ministry), a text which enlarges a little on what 'among you' means. It presents Jesus' diatribe against the Pharisees who sit on the seat of Moses, and whose authority is to that extent to be respected, but their example by no means to be followed, namely the way in which they parade and use their authority:

> But you are not to be called rabbi, for you have one teacher, and you are all brethren. And call no man your father on earth, for you have one Father, who is in heaven. Neither be called masters, for you have one master, the Christ. He who is greatest among you shall be your servant; whoever exalts himself will be humbled, and whoever humbles himself will be exalted.

Things must be different in the Christian community of the kingdom (in the community in which and for which Matthew is writing his gospel), because 'you are all brethren'. This text is the chief but by no means the only authority for my contention that Christian churches, or communities of believers, are essentially brotherhoods, and not 'essentially' hierarchical societies. It is also the authority for my deep reserve about the whole concept of *magisterium*: 'neither be called masters (Latin *magistri*), for you have one master, the Christ'. The concept is not simply to be rejected just because of Jesus' uncompromising and stark way of putting things; *that* I concede. But it is to be treated with the critical reserve and hesitation that Augustine will exhibit towards it, as we shall see below in Chapter 6. In a genuine brotherhood, authority—whether for teaching or governing—simply cannot be the same sort of thing as in a stratified secular society.

c. *Luke 22:24–32*

This passage from Luke is similar to our first from Mark, but in such a different context that it deserves quotation by itself. The context is the Last Supper, and Luke's account has certain slight affinities with John's, which can be referred to as a kind of commentary.

A dispute also arose among them, which of them was to be regarded as the greatest. And he said to them, 'The kings of the Gentiles exercise lordship over them; and those in authority over them are called benefactors. But not so with you; rather let the greatest among you become as the youngest, and the leader as one who serves. For which is the greater, one who sits at table, or one who serves? Is it not the one who sits at table? But I am among you as one who serves.

'You are those who have continued with me in my trials; as my Father appointed a kingdom for me, so do I appoint for you that you may eat and drink at my table in my kingdom, and sit on thrones judging the twelve tribes of Israel.

'Simon, Simon, behold Satan demanded to have you, that he might sift you like wheat, but I have prayed for you (singular) that your faith may not fail; and when you have turned again, strengthen your brethren.'

There are a few points to note here, in addition to the comments already made on the passage from Mark. First, the context; not only of the Last Supper and of Jesus' impending death, but of the eschatological hope to which this climax of his life (to serve and to give his life as a ransom for many) was being directed. There is table-fellowship now, in which he, 'Teacher and Lord' (Jn 13:13; Latin, *Magister et Dominus*) is among them as one that serves; and it foreshadows table-fellowship in the kingdom, where he will again be serving them (see Lk 12:37), and they will have seats of honour 'judging the twelve tribes of Israel'. The model of service is there all the time, even in the final glory of the kingdom; how much more in the preparation for that kingdom, in continuing with Jesus in his trials, through the eucharistic fellowship which is the very sacrament of his own supreme act of service, his giving of his life!

It does appear that in the kingdom the apostles will have a real 'hierarchical' pre-eminence, because they will be seated on twelve thrones. But here caution is necessary. The English word 'throne' has become almost exclusively associated with royalty; kings sit on thrones, and if we also now talk of bishops' thrones, it is because we have long assimilated bishops to kings (and the pope to a kind of king of kings). But the Greek word *thronos* did not necessarily have that limited and exalted connotation, any more than the English 'chair', though it can signify the presidency of a gathering. The key word in this passage, I suggest, is 'judging'. The apostles are going to have a position and a role fulfilling that of the ancient judges of Israel. And the judges were charismatic leaders of an egalitarian Israel organised (if one can call it organisation) in fraternal clans; an Israel to which the idea of monarchy, in effect of a 'hierarchical society', was abhorrent (see Judges 8:22–23, the whole story of Abimelech in Judges 9, and 1 Sam 8). But in the new Israel the charism of the new judges will be supremely the charism of service, of self-enslavement to the brotherhood, on the model of Christ the king himself.

The second point concerns the words that Jesus addressed to Simon—'Satan has desired to have you all (plural), to sift you all like wheat; but I have prayed for you in particular (singular)' etc. This is one of the classic texts adduced in support of the Petrine and papal primacy, together with Mt 16:16–19 and Jn 21:15–17. I do not deny the validity of this use of these texts, but I do maintain that it should be qualified, in a way it never is by ultramontanes, by a consideration of the contexts. All three contexts have Jesus rebuke Peter, or put him down more or less severely; do not his successors need to take these rebukes to heart in their manner of exercising the authority they base on these texts? Surely the proponents of extreme papalism should acknowledge the justice of this point.

But more precisely, with this particular text, Jesus addresses Simon immediately after expressly repudiating the models of earthly sovereignty, lordship and authority for the organisation of his kingdom; immediately after promising the twelve that they would sit on twelve thrones, without the slightest suggestion that any one throne would be pre-eminent over the others—perhaps they would be arranged in a circle, or round a round table. And finally he enjoins on Peter, when he is converted (and he will need conversion) the duty of confirming his *brethren*—not his subjects, but his brothers. What he does, in fact, as Gregory the Great perceived (the greatest and noblest, perhaps, of all the bishops of Rome), is confer on Peter the title and office of *servus servorum Dei*—the slave (not just the servant) of the slaves of God. If this title had ever been given the juridical, constitutional weight it deserves, instead of such titles as 'sovereign pontiff', 'his Holiness', 'Holy Father', which have no warrant whatsoever in the New Testament, then we would never have been burdened with the aberration of extreme ultramontane magisterial papalism.

2. Authority = *potestas* = *exousia*

Quite apart from Jesus' redefinition of authority in terms of service, there is enough evidence from the New Testament use of the word to rule out the centurion's military understanding of authority as a simple matter of 'go-and-he-goeth, come-and-he-cometh, do-this-and-he-doth-it' (Mt 8:9; Lk 7:8). This is the simple chain-of-command view of authority, in which command comes downward and answerability (responsibility) goes upward, so that the person at the top gives commands to everyone and is answerable to no one; the person at the bottom gives commands to no one and is answerable to every one above him; and those in the middle, like the centurion, have their authority over their subordinates confirmed by their responsibility to their superiors. It is a form of authority that is effective and necessary in armed forces and ships' crews (though it presupposes a professional competence at the top that is not always there). But it is more of a hindrance than a help to effectiveness in more complex societies, and is totally out of place in a fraternal society like the Church. It seems, however, to be the concept of authority entertained by magisterial papalists.

So what are the facts of New Testament usage? The Latin word used for authority is *potestas*; this is a legal or juridical word, unlike *potentia* which means sheer power or strength, without any associated idea of legality or right. A tyrant or usurper or bandit may have plenty of *potentia*, but his *potestas* is denied by law-abiding people. In the New Testament *potestas* nearly always translates the Greek *exousia*, and *exousia* is nearly always translated by *potestas*. *Potestas* is used 101 times for *exousia*, including five times rendering the Greek verbs *exousiazō* and *katexousiazō*. In the other direction, *exousia* is translated 96 times by *potestas*, and only once by another word, *licentia* (English, 'right'). So we can say that if we examine the meanings of *exousia* in the New Testament we will have a proper theological control for the notion of *potestas* as developed in the Latin, Roman Catholic Church.

I distinguish five variations in the basic meaning of 'lawfulness' which *exousia* has from the impersonal verb *exesti*:
(i) *lawful authority* or jurisdiction, enjoyed for example by Satan, Herod, Pilate, Christ, God;[1]
(ii) *authorisation*, licence (as with, e.g., a driving licence)—see that single translation of it by *licentia*;[2] this means the *right* to do things,

freedom of action, something that can be enjoyed by those under as well as those in authority. We may reasonably comment that to have *authority* is to have *liberty*, and conversely to have *liberty* is to have *authority*;

(iii) *authority in teaching*, signifying the right to teach, like the right to make laws, rather than just impressive competence in teaching. When it is said that Jesus taught with *exousia* and not like the scribes (Mt 7:29), it does not mean that he was a good teacher and they were bad ones; it means he taught like one laying down the law, like a new Moses (it is said at the end of the Sermon on the Mount), while they taught like men commenting on the law;

(iv) authority in the *concrete* sense, as in English 'the authorities', 'the powers that be'. Often here the lawfulness of these authorities is dubious; they are simply the powers, legitimate or not, and celestial/infernal powers as well as earthly ones;[3]

(v) lastly, it can sometimes mean sheer power or strength, the muscle or fire-power of these 'authorities'. But even in this case it is always used of *moral* beings, human, superhuman or divine (so that *exousia* is always subject to moral assessment), never of merely physical or impersonal power, force or strength. Thus if you were to talk of the *exousia* of a storm, say, or a volcano, you would be personifying these natural forces, just as you would be in English if you talked of their 'authority'.[4]

Thus *exousia* is primarily a term of law, sometimes one of politics or social ethics. But I would stress sense (ii), which it has more frequently than in the one case in which it is translated *licentia*. This correlation of authority with liberty or right shows that the centurion's military model of authority (which would be the dominant model in the absolutist military dictatorship that the Roman Empire had become and would remain to the end) is not in fact a just projection of *exousia* as the writers of the New Testament used the term and the earliest Greek-speaking Christian Churches understood it.

B. The distribution of authority

In investigating what the New Testament has to tell us on this subject, we will not be limited to its actual use of the word *exousia*, or its derivatives. There are things said about authority—most obviously in the so-called Petrine texts—where the word is not used at all. We shall see what the New Testament has to say about the distribution of authority under four headings: authority as possessed by God and Jesus Christ; authority as bestowed on the Church at large, or on the disciples of Christ in general; authority as bestowed on the apostles; and authority as bestowed on Peter. We shall observe, though, that this arrangement is a little artificial, because it was not, presumably, in the minds of the writers—the distinctions will often be blurred.

1. The authority of God and Christ

It is taken for granted that God (the Father) enjoys *exousia*, and so this truth is not mentioned as often as one might expect. However we learn in passing that he has *exousia* to cast into gehenna (Lk 12:5; translated 'power' in the RSV); he reserves the times and seasons of the last things to his own *exousia* (Acts 1:7); he has the same sort of *exousia* over his creatures as the potter over his clay (Rom 9:21; RSV 'right'). The distinctions made in the meaning of *exousia* in other contexts perhaps hardly apply to God. We could say that his *exousia* is the *ex*pression towards his creation of his own *ousia* or being; it is 'the good spreading itself abroad', *bonum diffusivum sui*.

Exousia is much more frequently ascribed to Christ. On the one hand his is a total and cosmic *exousia*, equal, indeed identical to the Father's; on the other hand it has been *given* to him (Mt 28:18). It is from the Father, as he is from the Father in his own *ousia*. So now, and in all further declensions of *exousia*, the *ex*- may be taken as signifying the fact of the authority in question being derived, received from another (ultimately from God, immediately from Christ).

Christ's *exousia* is also displayed before us in time, so that we do see it distinguished into the various senses listed above. He has the juridical *exousia* to forgive sins (Mt 9:6), to teach (Mt 7:29), to give commandments, to send his disciples, to judge (Jn 5:27). He has it in supreme measure in subjecting the cosmic *exousiai* to himself (Eph 1:21). He has the *exousia* of sheer divine power in doing miracles and casting out spirits (Mk 1:27). All this we may call his public or sovereign *exousia* as Messiah, as head of his body the Church.

But he also exercises a sort of private or personal *exousia*, which we could regard as his personal *licence* or liberty from the Father to do things as saviour, redeemer and high priest; the *exousia* to cleanse the Temple—the high priests asked him by what authority he does it (Mt 21:23), where one could equally well translate 'by what right'; the *exousia* above all to lay down his life and take it up again (Jn 10:18; RSV 'power'). This, surely, is his *ministerial* authority.

2. The authority bestowed on the Church in all its members

The crucial text in support of the ministerial collegialist insistence that *all* Christians, and not just the hierarchy, have been given a share in the authority of Christ, is Jn 1:12:

> But to all who received him, who believed in his name, he gave power to become children of God; who were born, not of blood nor of the will of the flesh nor of the will of man, but of God.

The word here translated 'power' by the RSV is *exousia*, *potestas* in the Latin. And 'power', though not wrong, is not quite adequate either. John is talking about more than an ability to become children of God; he means the *right* to become children of God, and as we have seen, right or liberty is a co-ordinate of authority.

Especially the right or authority of children, of sons. John does not mean either (in this context) that we have the right to become the infants, the babies of God. Most frequently in the New Testament being a child or son is contrasted, not with being an adult but with being a slave—a contrast taken for granted in the ancient world in a way that it no longer is with us. Let us bring in Paul to comment on John, with another crucial text, Gal 4:4–7:

> But when the time had fully come, God sent forth his Son, born of woman, born under the law, to redeem those who were under the law, so that we might receive adoption as sons. And because you are sons, God has sent the Spirit of his Son into our hearts, crying, 'Abba! Father!' So through God you are no longer a slave but a son, and if a son then an heir.

The word translated 'adoption as sons' would be better rendered as 'sonship by adoption'. What Paul surely means, and what John too implies, is that we receive a share in the divine sonship of Jesus Christ, with the difference (the only difference) that he is Son of God by nature, we share in that sonship by adoption. Now Christ, the Word made flesh of Jn 1, is not the baby son of God; as the Only-begotten he is *equal* to the Father. So as we, the faithful, all baptised Christians, share in his divine sonship, we also share in his equality, and therefore in his authority.

We should also consider those texts which talk of the faithful, or the Church sharing in the priesthood of Christ. Actually, they talk about sharing in his *royal* priesthood, or even more definitely in both his kingship and his priesthood: 1 Pet 2:5, 9 and Rev 1:6; 5:10. These texts are applying to the Church, the new people of God, the special privilege that made Israel God's uniquely chosen people in Exod 19:6. For us the simple point is that both priest-hood and kingship are authority roles. If we share in Christ's priesthood and his kingship, we share in his royal authority and his sacerdotal authority.

3. The authority bestowed on the apostles

On this point there is no difference of opinion between the MPs and the MCs, so we need not examine texts in detail to establish that Christ did bestow his authority on the apostles. But there are one or two observations to be made. The first is that texts adduced in support are not always quite as explicit or unambiguous as they are assumed to be; that is, it is not always clear whether the persons referred to are exclusively the apostles, or the disciples in general. This is particularly the case with Mt 18, usually con-sidered a discourse to the apostles. It is in fact addressed to 'the disciples' (18:1). Now it is true that Matthew often does mean the apostles by 'the disciples' (10:1, 11:1). But if we treat this follow-ing text as a whole—which we clearly ought to do—it will surely seem rather odd to take some verses as applying only to the apostles and others as applying (as they are always assumed to do) to all the disciples. There are sentences, in other words, that a natural reading forbids us to restrict to the apostles; so should we so restrict any of them? Here is Mt 18:15–20;

> If your brother sins against you, go and tell him his fault between him and you alone. If he listens to you, you have gained your brother. But if he does not listen, take one or two others along with you, that every word may be con-firmed by the evidence of two or three witnesses. If he refuses to listen to them, tell it to the church; and if he refuses to listen even to the church, let him be to you as a Gentile and a tax collector. Truly I say to you, whatever you bind on earth shall be bound in heaven, and whatever you loose on earth shall be loosed in heaven. Again I say to you,

if two of you agree on earth about anything they ask, it will
be done for them by my Father in heaven. For where two or
three are gathered in my name, there am I in the midst of
them.

Now it is evident that the 'you' of the first few verses (singular
in the Greek) does not just refer to any one of the apostles only; the
Christian disciple in general is being addressed. And we are being
addressed, individually, in the context of 'the church', i.e. the
community of believers in any particular place. We have here,
what is probably true of nearly all the teaching in this gospel, a
piece of our Lord's teaching as it had been digested in and applied
to themselves by the Christian communities in which and for
which Matthew was writing. In this case it was on the problem of
how to settle disputes or grievances within the community. And
the final arbiter is 'the church'. Then the last two sentences, about
'two of you' and 'two or three of you', are also hardly to be
applied to the apostles alone. They seem to be explaining the verse
for which the first verses had been providing the context, v. 18,
the climax of the passage about binding and loosing, i.e. about
authority. So it would seem that neither can v. 18 be reasonably
treated as applying to the apostles alone. It is most reasonably to
be taken as applying precisely to 'the church', i.e. to the local
community.

But of course there are passages in which Jesus is explicitly
bestowing authority on the twelve apostles, for example Mt 10.
And my second observation is concerned, in particular, with Mt
10:1:

And he called to him his twelve disciples and gave them
authority (*exousia/potestas*) over unclean spirits, to cast them
out, and to heal every disease and every infirmity.

Now the authority in question here does not seem to be authority
within the community of believers, over the faithful; it is an
authority over forces of evil, over 'the world', in which the
faithful will share, according to the charisms of the Spirit. It could
be dubbed a charismatic authority (cf. 1 Cor 12:7–11, 28). It is
true, the chapter ends (Mt 10:40) 'He who receives you receives
me', and receiving appears to mean 'accepting the teaching of', so
a kind of authority among and over those who receive the apostles
may reasonably be inferred.

But it is inferred, not explicitly stated. That the first Christians
worried about such authority and the status that normally goes

with it is clear from the number of times the disciples are revealed wrangling about 'who should be the greatest'. But the answer they receive from Jesus is invariably the same: 'Stop wrangling', in effect, 'about trivia, about such childish baubles. Instead of being so childish about status and protocol and who should be king of the castle, become like children, be little in your own eyes, be each other's servants and slaves—because you are all, in fact, brethren.' It seems that he could not care less about arranging 'a hierarchy'.

4. The authority bestowed on Peter

That Jesus bestowed a special authority on Peter is also not in dispute between MPs and MCs. What we MCs do contest is the exaggeration of the special Petrine authority by MPs. We shall deal with that in the next section of this chapter. But here I just want to suggest that there are Petrine texts that are not sufficiently exploited even by MPs, texts moreover which imply, when carefully interpreted, that the authority bestowed on Peter continued to be a reality among the Churches even after his death—though they do not specify that it would be located in the Church of Rome.

The first is a text that is indeed classically referred to in support of the Petrine authority, but not quite in this sense—Jn 21. Raymond E. Brown, in *The Community of the Beloved Disciple*,[5] presents a convincing, carefully worked out picture of the Johannine type of Christian community from its beginnings until the Johannine epistles were written, about AD 100. According to his reconstruction it was a type of community that had very little interest in structures or institutional authority, and thought until almost the very end, when it was being torn apart by internal dissensions, that it could really do without them. But he goes on to suggest that ch. 21—written of course long after Peter's death, and also some years after the rest of Jn and the Johannine epistles—shows a spokesman of this type of community accepting the need for, as well as the reality of, some kind of institutionalised apostolic Petrine authority. So Jesus' conversation with Peter in this chapter about 'feeding my sheep' is not just evidence that Peter was given this authority by Christ; it is evidence that the reality and the necessity of this authority is being asserted after Peter's death by Christian communities traditionally inclined to insist on their own, idiosyncratic, independence. The enigmatic remarks that follow about the beloved disciple indicate, however, that the writer continues to insist that there are dimensions and values of Christian life not subject to any human authority.

The other text is 2 Pet 1. If the practically unanimous opinion of the scholars is correct, that this epistle is the latest of the New Testament writings (as late as AD 120 according to some), and is pseudonymously attributed to Peter, then I think it can only mean that the writer and the type of community he represented considered that 'Peter' in some way or other lived on in the Churches as an authority after Peter's death. He is not just trying to claim an apostle's authority for his own teaching, as could be said about the writer of the pastoral epistles (Timothy and Titus), on the common assumption that that was not Paul himself. 2 Peter contains very little of that sort of teaching. But it does emphasise in 1:12–15 the need for something, not specified, to maintain the Petrine tradition after Peter's death:

> Therefore I intend always to remind you of these things, though you know them and are established in the truth that you have. I think it right, as long as I am in this body, to arouse you by way of reminder, since I know that the putting off of my body will be soon, as our Lord Jesus Christ showed me. And I will see to it that after my departure you may be able at any time to recall these things.

It looks like a kind of apologia for some sort of succession to Peter's authority, the nature of which would have been more specifically obvious to the writer and his contemporary readers than it is to us.

5. Summary

The case then of Christian ecclesial authority, as the New Testament presents it, may be summed up as follows:

(i)   The divine fullness of authority (*plenitudo potestatis* or *plena potestas* in juridical terms) belongs to Jesus Christ, the head of the Church;

(ii)   this authority, like the other privileges and titles of Christ, is participated in by the whole Church and all its members. The whole body of the faithful, therefore, shares in Christ's *plena potestas*, to the extent that they enjoy 'the authority to become children of God', and are sons of God in the Son, and are free with the freedom with which Christ has made us free (Gal 5:1), the glorious liberty of the children of God (Rom 8:21);

(iii)   it is also participated in fully by the apostles, or by the leaders of the Christian communities who are the heirs of the apostles; they too share in Christ's *plena potestas* not just as members of the Church but as apostles, leaders, bishops;

(iv)   Finally, it is shared in fully by Peter, by the one man who is the focus of unity of all the communities, of all the Churches; and he and his successors or heirs enjoy the *plena potestas* not just as Christians, not just as apostles or bishops, but as Peter, as bishops of Rome or popes.

But the first participation is the primary and fundamental one, and is *in no sense* abrogated by or dependent on the two subsequent participations. They are, rather, its instruments and servants. The authority of the whole Church and all its members, their *plena potestas*, is derived immediately from Christ through faith (and baptism/confirmation), and is at the service of the world. The *plena potestas* of the bishops, derived immediately from Christ, is at the service of this universal ecclesial authority; and so is the *plena potestas*, the special Petrine authority of the pope, which is also derived immediately from Christ.

About how these three funds, as it were, of *plena potestas* were to be co-ordinated, there is no evidence that Christ laid down any rules at all. In the next section we shall see how the first Christian communities, which we meet in the New Testament, drew on them. One thing we can say for certain, and that is that the ministerial collegialist solution, which would give full value to all of them, is more congenial to the New Testament model than the magisterial papalist one which so exaggerates the Petrine authority of the pope that the apostolic authority of the bishops becomes a pale wraith of its former self, and the 'discipular' or ecclesial authority of the whole Church and of all the faithful disappears without trace.

C. The deployment of authority

Two general remarks must be made to begin with about authority. First, it is important to distinguish between the possession of authority and the exercise of authority. Exercise, of course, presupposes possession, but possession does not necessarily lead to, or require exercise. Authority is possessed in order to be available for exercise as and when required. But very often authority that is possessed should not, and occasionally even cannot be exercised. Let me illustrate with a secular case: Queen Elizabeth II of Great

Britain and Northern Ireland has in law the same authority as Queen Elizabeth I of England and Ireland. That is to say, she is the sovereign, the fount not only of honour but of law and justice in her dominions. But she cannot and may not personally exercise this authority in the same way or to the same extent as that formidable lady, her namesake.

Now for an ecclesiastical illustration, working in the opposite direction: Eleutherius and Cornelius, bishops of Rome at the end of the second and in the middle of the third century, had exactly the same fullness of authority as Pius XII and John Paul II, bishops of Rome in the twentieth century. But they did not exercise, and could not have exercised it in the same way or to the same extent. The point is worth making against the ultramontane MPs who tend to maintain both that the present style and quantity of exercising the papal authority is of its essence, and that (this is popular MP mythology) it always has been exercised in this way. The last point receives trivial, but illuminating, verification from the current English breviary—a post-Vatican II document, be it noted. In the old Latin breviary readings from ancient authors used to be headed 'From a sermon of St Augustine, bishop', or 'From a sermon of St Leo the Great, pope', or 'From the letters of St Catherine, virgin'—in other words every holy writer was given his or her appropriate rank, and of course among these ranks there was that of pope. The current English translation of the new breviary, being modern, has dropped this preoccupation with status, and we now have 'From a sermon of St Augustine', or 'From the letters of St Catherine', and from the New Testament we have readings from 'the letter of St Paul to the Romans' instead of the old-fashioned 'the letter of St Paul the apostle to the Romans'. *But* there is one exception to this modern levelling process: popes! Popes are so important, and always have been so important, that their status remains, and is now given even greater emphasis. So we have readings 'From the letter of Pope St Clement I' or 'From the sermons of Pope St Leo the Great'. Someone's being pope, it seems, is more important than his being a saint, and certainly more important than Paul's being an apostle. As I said, a trivial but illuminating case of modern papolatry, founded on papal mythology.

This particular case against MP ultramontanism may be put briefly in logical form: if a concentration of decisive control over the Church in the hands of the pope is necessarily implied by the dogmatically defined doctrine of papal primacy, then that concentration of control must have been wielded by popes from St Peter onwards; but it was not wielded by popes from St Peter onwards; therefore it is not necessarily implied by the doctrine of papal primacy. If you deny the consequent, you deny the antecedent.

My second remark is that for authority that is possessed to be exercised it has to be institutionalised. For exercise it requires some formal structures. What we shall see here, and in the next chapter, is that the actual power wielded by the possessors of the three 'funds' of *plena potestas* has grown or shrunk in the course of Church history in proportion to the degree of structural institutionalisation they have achieved. Here we will be examining that deployment of authority as evidenced in the pages of the New Testament.

1. Varieties of structure in the first Christian communities

We have already referred to Raymond E. Brown's work, *The Community of the Beloved Disciple*, in which he investigates the type of community from which the Johannine writings of the New Testament emerged and for which they were composed. He found these communities to be rather inward-turning, identifying themselves by their stress on love of the brotherhood and the guidance of the Holy Spirit, and more negatively by their hostility to 'the Jews' (meaning those who did not believe in Christ) and 'the world' (meaning Gentiles who did not receive him). He also found, as we saw, that they seemed to have had very little interest in structures or institutional authority.

His is one of a number of recent studies devoted to reconstructing as far as possible the kind of community from and for which other books of the New Testament were written. And the general consensus is that these early communities differed from each other very widely indeed. We have to bear in mind that they were all, for several decades, very small, about the size, not of a modern parish, but of a modern parish congregation, though much more cohesive.[6] Nor would they all have been founded by an apostle like Paul. Of the Churches to which Paul wrote letters, for instance, those of Rome and Colossae were certainly not founded by him, or by any of the apostles as far as we know. The Church of Rome certainly existed before either Paul or Peter ever reached the city.

So these little churches would spontaneously have adopted

very different kinds of community organisation, though it is equally true that because of their close fraternal contacts with each other they would have been mutually influencing each other all the time. In the Acts of the Apostles Luke gives us an idea of how most Churches were organised, or how he thought they should be organised, at the time he wrote, say about AD 80; he puts this pattern back forty years or so to the beginnings. Lucan Churches were modelled on Jewish synagogues (nothing more natural), and run by 'presbyters' or elders (Acts 14:23). The author would have it that this was an apostolic institution. It may have been, but it is equally likely that it was originally an institution of the Church in Jerusalem (Acts 15:2, 6, 22) which spread to other Churches; the two possibilities do not exclude each other. The synagogue model was in any case modified in some places by other secular models, or even ones taken from pagan religious institutions. Thus at Ephesus (Acts 20:17, 28) the elders of the Church are also called its guardians (RSV for *episkopoi*, meaning 'overseers' or 'superintendents', who will later become 'bishops'). Paul addresses his letter to the Philippians (a Church he certainly founded) 'to all the saints in Christ Jesus who are at Philippi, with the bishops (these same *episkopoi*—I don't know why RSV is not consistent and doesn't call them 'guardians' here too) and deacons' (Phil 1:1); no mention of elders at all.

We find the same sort of organisation in the Churches for which the pastoral epistles were written, not very long, probably, after Acts; deacons, elders, bishops (guardians) are all mentioned, and elders and bishops seem again to be the same persons (Tit 1:5–7). 1 Pet 5:1ff. also testifies to it. So we can conclude that most early Churches soon developed a system of government by elders—in fact a 'presbyterian' system.

But there were, apparently, notable exceptions besides the Johannine Churches already mentioned. Thus Paul's two letters to the Corinthians give us a fairly full picture of life in that Church, life that could have done with some firm regulation by such officials as elders and guardians, and yet not once are they mentioned. What are mentioned in 1 Cor 12 are a great variety of charisms, including those of 'helpers' and 'administrators' (literally, 'governings': 12:28) which would elsewhere be the responsibilities of deacons and elders. But here they are gifts of the Holy Spirit, and these alone are seen as articulating the Christian community, the Church, as the body of Christ.

But whatever the organisation of a Church, whether by an

ordained ministry of deacons and elders/guardians or by a more various charismatic ministry (or indeed both), these Churches were small enough to ensure that their mere existence as communities of faith provided what I called the general or ecclesial fund of authority, given by Christ to all who believe in him, with the minimal structure necessary to enable it to be exercised. To New Testament evidence of its exercise, along with the two other funds, the apostolic and the Petrine, let us now turn.

2. The deployment of authority in the New Testament

a. *Acts 1:15–26 and 6:1–6*

First consider the episode of filling the vacancy in the apostolic college left by the defection of Judas (Acts 1:15–26). It must be surprising to true ultramontane MPs that Peter did not anticipate the new Code of Canon Law and just appoint a successor to Judas on his own authority. After all, he was the sovereign pontiff, was he not, the sole vicar of Christ, enjoying alone the *plenitudo potestatis*? But he didn't do that. As Peter, the Rock (no longer Simon), he took the lead, but he involved the whole community in the decision. And the way Luke tells the story, the decision to leave the final choice to the Holy Spirit did not come from any suggestion of Peter's, so one presumes it came from the floor of the house.

A similar procedure was followed in the appointment of the first assistants to the apostles, whom tradition—but not St Luke —calls deacons (Acts 6:1–6).

b. *Acts 15*

The so-called Council of Jerusalem is a much more interesting instance. First of all it shows us the relationship of the two particular Churches, that of Antioch and that of Jerusalem. Jerusalem is the mother Church, allowed a kind of authority analogous to that which was fairly soon to be accorded to the Church of Rome. And it seems to be members of this Church who by their officious intervention in Antioch caused all the trouble (Acts 15:1–2). It is true that Luke says it was people coming from Judaea, not precisely from Jerusalem. But it almost certainly means the same thing; in a similar incident Paul talks of people coming 'from James', who presided over the Jerusalem Church, as we know from this chapter of Acts (see Gal 2:12 and *c.* below).

But the Church of Antioch on the one hand does not take this interference lying down, and on the other continues to recognise the authority of the Church of Jerusalem. They send a deputation which includes Paul and Barnabas 'to go up to Jerusalem to the apostles and the elders about this question'. So that is where the leading authority is felt to lie, with the apostles and the elders. In the debate Peter takes the lead and suggests the line to be followed (supporting Paul and Barnabas) (15:7–11); then James, who was in effect the bishop of Jerusalem, sums up and makes a concrete proposal (15:13–21); and finally and most illuminating of all, this proposal 'seemed good to the apostles and the elders, *with the whole Church*' (15:22). How the whole Church took part in the discussion, or indicated its approval of the final proposal, we are not told. But its participation in the decision, hence its authority or right to participate, is clearly if briefly acknowledged. If we are going to take this as a kind of New Testament model for councils of the Church, it suggests that such councils are not limited in membership by divine law to bishops.

c. Galatians 2:11–21

It is worth examining the passage referred to above from Galatians 2 about Peter's exercise of his authority. It is the occasion when Paul 'opposed Cephas to the face'. Peter, the possessor of the Petrine authority, was wrong, having given in to pressure from the conservative old guard, and Paul, not even one of the twelve, was right. But equally important, I think, is that Paul withstood Peter to the face in the presence of the community at Antioch, and that Peter admitted his mistake and returned to his earlier practice of eating with the Gentiles.[7] All the more honour to him. If Peter could be wrong on a matter of such vital importance to the very survival of the Church of Christ, Peter the rock on which that Church is built, and could admit and rectify his mistake, then presumably the Holy See after him can be equally wrong, and should find it no diminution of its authority and *magisterium*—if you want to use the word—to admit it.

d. Acts 10:1 – 11:18

In Acts 10 Peter takes a truly Petrine initiative and goes and baptises Cornelius and his household. The initiative, of course, is

really God's, but Peter is 'obedient to the vision'. From our point
of view the interesting thing is what happens when he goes back
to Jerusalem (11:2–4):

> So when Peter went up to Jerusalem, the circumcision party
> criticised him saying, 'Why did you go to uncircumcised
> men and eat with them?' But Peter began and explained to
> them in order . . .

The point is, Peter does not dispute their right to call him to
account for an important decision he had made on his own
authority. He acknowledges, implicitly, that as a man, as one of
the brethren, he is responsible or answerable to the brotherhood
for his exercise of the authority, which he has indeed received
from Christ and not from the brotherhood, but which he has
received for the sake of the brotherhood and exercises within the
brotherhood. This is because the brotherhood has also received
authority from Christ—and not from Peter. In this case Peter
seems to be rather more modest about his authority than the
circumcision party is about theirs. He sets an excellent example
that should be incorporated in any Petrine theology.

NOTES

1 Satan, Lk 4:6; 22:53; Eph 2:2;
   Herod, Lk 23:7;
   Pilate, Lk 20:20; Jn 19:10, 11;
   Christ and God, see below.
It may seem surprising to talk of Satan having a *lawful* authority, yet this
is a common idea among the Fathers, with biblical support. We see God
giving Satan authority of a sort over Job (Job 1:12; 2:6). But more than
that, man has sold himself to the devil by sin, so that the devil now has the
authority over us of a master over his slaves. God wishing to redeem
mankind, is morally obliged to do just that—to buy us back, or—this is
Augustine's more subtle way of putting it—to manoeuvre Satan in a
battle of wits into forfeiting his authority over us by cheating, which he
does by engineering the unmerited death of the innocent Christ.
2 1 Cor 8:9, the right of the Corinthians, as free in Christ, to eat any
meats without scruple. But *exousia* is used in practically this sense in far
more cases than this solitary instance, most strikingly in Jn 10:18 (RSV
'power').
3 Rom 13:1–3, Eph 1:21, 3:10, 6:12, Col 1:16.
4 Col 1:13 (RSV 'the dominion of darkness'). Perhaps this text illus-

trates the *exousia* of Satan, like Lk 22:53, where it is translated 'the power of darkness'. In each case, however, 'darkness' is being personified.

5 Raymond E. Brown, *The Community of the Beloved Disciple* (Paulist Press, New York/Geoffrey Chapman, London, 1979).

6 In Acts 2:41, Luke gives the numbers of believers as 3,000 and in 4:4 as 5,000. But these numbers are almost certainly symbolic, representing the Church as the new Israel (cf. also the numbers fed in the gospels on the loaves and fishes); and even if they are taken literally, most of those converted on these occasions would not be inhabitants of Jerusalem, but pilgrims come up for the feasts. So back home they would form only small groups.

7 To be sure, the text does not say this explicitly. But the alternative inference, that Peter persisted in withdrawing from 'table-fellowship' with the Gentiles (which would mean not sharing in the eucharist with them), and thus in effect severed communion with Paul, is scarcely tenable. That Paul withstood Peter to the face in public, in the presence of the Antioch Church—or the Jewish portion of it—is also pretty certain. It was, after all, a public issue.

3

AUTHORITY
IN THE CHURCH
IN THE FIRST MILLENNIUM

We now go on to consider the development of structures of authority in the Church during its first thousand years. The symbolic end of this period, as I see it, is not the year AD 1000 but AD 1054, which marks the definitive break between Rome and Constantinople, between the Latin Christianity of the West and the Greek Christianity of the East. It is not only the structures of authority that are developing all the time, but also the very concept of it. But that kind of development will engage our attention more in the next chapter.

Our period naturally divides into two parts—the first three hundred years, during which Christianity was an illicit and therefore sporadically persecuted religion in the Roman Empire; and the centuries following the conversion of Constantine, during which Catholic Christianity was (for the most part) the official and only recognised religion of the Empire, and of the new kingdoms that succeeded it in western and northern Europe.

A. Structures of authority in the Church up to AD 325

1. The evolution of episcopacy

We saw in the last chapter, section C.1, that the Churches of the New Testament differed from one another widely in organisation, and that in those governed by an ordained ministry there was no distinction between *presbyteroi* and *episkopoi*, elders and supervisors. The first, I suggested, was a title of status, the second one of function. So these Churches would have effectively been managed by a committee of elders—they would have had a 'presbyterian' type of organisation.

But by the second half of the second century—by AD 175 at the

latest—*episkopoi*, whom we can now call bishops without in-
accuracy, were everywhere quite distinct from *presbyteroi*, whom
we cannot yet without anachronism call priests, and everywhere
Churches are governed, or presided over, each by a single bishop,
assisted by a variable number of presbyters and deacons. A presbyterian structure has evolved into an episcopal one. The earliest
evidence for this is to be found in the letters of Ignatius of Antioch
from the second decade of the second century, letters he wrote to
a number of Churches round the Aegean Sea, as he was on his
way, a prisoner, from Antioch in Syria, where he had been
bishop, to Rome to be thrown to the lions in the Colosseum. His
letters show that the episcopal structure was well enough established in these Churches to have acquired a justifying theology—
or perhaps it still had enough opponents for Ignatius to feel he had
to justify it theologically. But they do not show that it was yet
universal.

How and why did this gradual switch from a presbyteral to an
episcopal structure take place? The classical treatment of the subject is Bishop Lightfoot's *Dissertation on the Christian Ministry*,
appended to his *Commentary on Philippians*, first published in
1868.[1] On this particular point he argues convincingly to two
conclusions: first that the model Church (and it is plausible
enough) was the Church of Jerusalem, and that in fact the Acts of
the Apostles presents us with the first bishop, in the developed
sense of the term, in the person of James, the brother of the Lord
(Acts 15:13). The institution would have been spontaneously
copied from Jerusalem by other Churches. Secondly he argues
that bishops evolved from presbyters by way of elevation, and
not from apostles by way of localisation. His point is that an
apostle, as one sent to preach, is by nature an itinerant missionary
preacher, whereas a bishop is by nature a resident pastor of a
particular local congregation or Church. There is nothing in the
nature of an apostle's vocation and function to turn him into a
resident pastor.

The most obvious successors to the precise apostolic function
of the apostles were the prophets mentioned by the *Didache*,[2]
probably the earliest Christian text outside the New Testament. It
had not been discovered and published when Lightfoot wrote his
dissertation. These prophets of the *Didache* seemed to be regarded
as superior to the resident *episkopoi/presbyteroi*, so that they took
precedence whenever they turned up in a community. But that is
the point: they turned up, and then went on their way again. They

were obliged to be wanderers. One way of telling a false prophet from a true one, says the *Didache*, was if he stayed with you more than three days! I suppose a poor prophet, if he grew weary of being perpetually on the move, could retire and settle down somewhere. But then, the presumption is, he would cease to be a prophet, and certainly would cease to have any claim to the precedence and respect that were accorded to prophets in those circles.

Daniélou[3] modifies Lightfoot's theory somewhat by suggesting that two parallel structures developed in the first decades of Church existence: the structure of a residential ministry on the lines sketched by Lightfoot, and the structure of an itinerant missionary ministry, supervised by apostles, under whom were 'prophets and teachers' (Acts 13:1), who are not, in his view, to be regarded as performing a purely charismatic ministry merely on the strength of 1 Cor 12:28.

The theory is attractive, but need concern us no further, since this special 'itinerant' ministry eventually faded away as an institutionalised structure. We are still left with a theological problem: if as Lightfoot argues and Daniélou tacitly agrees, bishops as we know them came into existence not as localised apostles but as elevated presbyters, how can they really be, as Catholic doctrine accepted by MCs as well as by MPs says they are, the successors of the apostles? The brief answer is that they are the successors or heirs (a better word, I think) to the *authority* of the apostles, though not to their specific apostolic *function*. A secular illustration, to which many parallels may be found, will indicate how this can be. The little principality of Andorra in the Pyrenees has as joint heads of state two Co-Princes, who are the bishop of Urgel in Spain and the President of the French Republic. How does the French President come by this archaic mediaeval position, which dates back to times centuries before there was a French Republic? It belongs to him precisely as successor or heir to the Bourbon kings of France, even though his is quite a different sort of office from theirs, just as the office of bishop is quite different from that of apostle.

But I don't think that this answer quite solves the matter. For it would appear from the historical evidence to be the case that bishops as we know them did not yet exist in many or most Churches when authority was passing from the apostles to people in a succeeding generation. To whom was it passing, then? It can only have been to those committees or bodies of elders/

presbyters/*episkopoi* who were presiding collectively over these Churches. So while it is descriptively true to say with Lightfoot that bishops are elevated presbyters—that the chairman of the committee eventually became a life-president of the Church assisted by a council—it would be doctrinally more correct to say that presbyters are demoted bishops. The members of what was originally a governing body, a collective leadership, were demoted to being the advisers of an individual governor.

The point becomes even more intriguing when we turn to the most important instance of apostolic succession—that of the bishops of Rome to the primatial authority of Peter. For the evidence is really very strong, though it is the evidence of silence, that the Church of Rome was not presided over by a bishop until about AD 140. That, at least, is the earliest date from which we have positive evidence for the existence of such an officer. In other words, the Church of Rome began, like other Churches, with a presbyteral structure of authority, and was far slower than almost all other Churches to change to the episcopal structure. The only other Church to take even longer to make the change was the second most important Church of the Christian world, that of Alexandria. It is Ignatius, with his very high doctrine of episcopacy, who provides us with the evidence from silence that when he was writing his letters, between 110 and 117, Rome was not an episcopal Church. In all his other letters he stresses the theological, the spiritual importance of the bishop and his authority. In his *Letter to the Roman Church*, to which he accords a unique respect as the Church to which the apostles Peter and Paul had given commandments, he never once mentions the bishop or the office of bishop.

If it was the case then (and it is a very strong case) that the Roman Church had a governing body of elders instead of a presiding bishop for anything up to eighty years after Peter's death, to whom did his primatial authority pass? One answer could be that it passed to the Roman Church as a whole, to the whole community of believers in Rome; another, more acceptable perhaps, that it passed to the governing body of elders, who eventually conformed to the prevailing custom of almost all the other Churches (perhaps bowing to popular pressure?), and conferred it on a life-president or bishop. In any case, all this raises the question of whether the so-called 'monarchical' espiscopate (I would prefer to call it 'presidential'), and especially the monarchical papacy, are essential to the hierarchical constitution of the

Church. If episcopacy and papacy were once, in the English constitutional parlance, held in commission,[4] could that not conceivably ever be the case again? It is something at least worth bearing in mind for ecumenical dialogue with non-episcopal Churches. If we episcopalians and papalists concede to them the possibility, they may be the more willing not to require of us the actuality, as a condition for organic reunion.

2. The development of synodal government

Although in the centuries under consideration there is ample and continuous evidence of a unique authority and pre-eminence being accorded to the Church of Rome and its bishops (after it acquired them), we cannot really talk about the development, or extension, or routine juridical exercise of a papal authority during this period. It is in fact something of an anachronism (or myth) to think of these early bishops of Rome as popes. If this was a title sometimes accorded them in affectionate respect (it only means 'daddy', after all), so it was to many other bishops. It is in the century after Nicaea that papal authority will be extended, institutionalised and justified theologically with great suddenness and thoroughness.

What is developed in the second and third centuries is synodal structures of government for the Churches. To begin with, as we remarked in the last chapter, there was really no overall organisation of the Churches into a universal Church; there were just Churches, local communities, in informal, though close, relationships of fraternal communion with each other. First the apostles, and then, on Daniélou's hypothesis, the itinerant missionary ministers, the prophets and teachers, would have exercised some general supervision. But eventually it was the bishops of the local Churches themselves who came to exercise this kind of authority by acting together in what they called regional synods or councils. Nowadays we call the same sort of thing episcopal conferences. In most regions or provinces of the Roman Empire (our knowledge of what happened outside its borders is rather scanty), the bishops would meet at least once a year, and deliberate on matters of common concern, such as doctrine and discipline, and regard themselves as individually bound by their common decisions.

I talked of 'synodal structures' in the plural, because this development was by no means uniform throughout the Christian world. What varied most from region to region was the primatial or presiding authority accorded to the bishops of certain Churches. Very commonly it would be the bishop of the Church in the provincial capital who was the permanent chairman of synod, or primate (a later title was 'metropolitan', and later still 'archbishop'). Such came to be the position of the bishop of Carthage in North Africa, or the bishop of Caesarea in Palestine. But two such metropolitans in particular, the bishop of Alexandria in Egypt and Cyrenaica, and the bishop of Rome in Italy south of the Rubicon and the islands of Sicily, Sardinia and Corsica, came to have a much greater authority in their regions than that of mere chairmen of synods. The bishops of lesser Churches in those regions were very much the subordinates of the primates, subject to their supervision and jurisdiction.

Thus, in this first period of the Church's history after New Testament times, we see what I called the apostolic/episcopal fund of authority clearly identified and strongly developed, and institutionalised especially in synodal forms of Church government. We see the Petrine/papal fund clearly identified in the Church of Rome and its bishop, but not otherwise very much developed. What I called the general fund, by which all the faithful participate in the authority of Christ, continues to be there, and to express itself in the life and above all in the devotional practices of the local Christian communities (e.g. in the cult of the martyrs and the care for the dead) but is not institutionalised apart from the role played by the faithful in the choice of their pastors and clergy. We know very little of what that role was. But I imagine it is safe to say that where Churches continued to be comparatively small communities, and closely knit, no bishop would last very long who did not enjoy the confidence and support of his flock. Bishops, we may take it, were on the whole genuinely representative of the faith and the sentiments of the Churches over which they presided.

B. Structures of authority in the Church, AD 325–1054

One supremely important element in the life of the Church that owes its origin entirely to lay initiative, to popular religion—i.e. to the general authority of the faithful at large—is monasticism. It started, traditionally, with St Anthony in Egypt in the late third century. But it really began to flourish and spread in the fourth century, after the peace of the Church. It was, to a great extent, a

spontaneous protest against the insidious worldliness with which
the Church was infected as a result of what we can fairly call the
Constantinian revolution.

For the conversion of Constantine (such as it was) and its effects
on the status and self-awareness of the *Catholica*, the great
Church, was indeed for the Church a cataclysmic revolution.
Within a century the Church passed from being an unlawful and
persecuted organisation to being the state Church, custodian of
the official religion, of the Roman Empire.

1. Some general effects of the Constantinian revolution

The most obvious result of the Church becoming a lawful organisation, and then from the time of Theodosius the Great (more
precisely from the Council of Constantinople, 381) becoming the
official state religion, was a rapid increase in the number of
Christians. Not only was it now quite safe to be a Christian, but
increasingly it became more and more unsafe—or at the best a
considerable disadvantage—not to be one. A large proportion of
such new Christians were naturally enough only nominal ones.
Inevitably the Church, and with it no doubt a number of its
clergy, even its bishops, became more worldly. It was against
such worldliness that the monastic movement staged its spontaneous and powerful protest.

Worldliness is not quite the same as secularity. One kind of
worldliness that is easily overlooked—we shall be looking at it
more closely in the next chapter—was rapid *sacralisation* of things
Christian and ecclesiastical. The ancient pagan (and Jewish)
world, and this included the Roman Empire and its political
structures, was an intensely sacred world; that is to say a world in
which the sacred was very clearly and awesomely and dangerous-
ly demarcated from the profane. Without the proper ritual precautions it was dangerous to pass from one to the other, and
everyday life was full of little boundaries, often unsuspected,
between the two. Now Christ in his preaching of the kingdom of
God, and his redemption of mankind from sin and the power of
the law, had deliberately and explicitly demolished the barrier
between the sacred and the profane. A symbol of this was the
tearing of the veil in the Temple when he died on the cross. So in
the Christian life and the Christian community no place, no time,
no person, no item of food or drink or clothing was more sacred
than any other; nothing was sacred and nothing was profane,

because everything and everyone that was good was 'holy to the Lord', and only sin and what is evil was unholy.

But with the Constantinian revolution this rapidly changes. The Roman world remains as sacred as it had been. But now Christianity and the Church become the bearers and custodians of the sacred in society, in the stead of the old pagan religion.

In fact the most profound, and in a sense natural, consequence of the Constantinian revolution was that the Church should simply become identified with civil society—should become civil society in its religious aspect, and that Catholic Christianity should simply become what sociologists of religion call 'the civil religion' of the Roman Empire.[5] This is almost certainly what Constantine and at least his immediate successors intended, and thought they were achieving. There were highly placed Christians who agreed with him, chief among them being Eusebius, bishop of Caesarea, the Church historian. He gave the appropriate ideo-theology its clearest (I am inclined to say its most horrifying) expression in his work *The Life of Constantine*. The emperor is for him a second David, sometimes called the thirteenth apostle, and the conversion of the empire to Christianity is practically identified with the definitive coming of the kingdom of God.

2. Particular effects of the Constantinian revolution on the structures of authority in the Church

With respect to its structures of authority (as in other respects) the Church partly succumbed to these pressures and was corrupted by them, and partly resisted and overcame them.

a. Loss of the authority bestowed on the faithful

The chief, and permanent casualty was what I have called the general fund of authority enjoyed by all the faithful. This happened in three ways.

First, the Church—experienced as co-terminous and practically identical with the empire—came to be experienced like the empire as a single, universal *institution*, as well as, and gradually more than a great number of local communities or Churches bound by little more than a fraternal sense of communion. Now in such a vast institution the masses, unless there are highly developed organs of representation which the ancient world simply lacked, can exercise little or no authority.

Secondly, we have noticed the rapid sacralisation of the Church and Christian life in the wake of the Constantinian revolution. This meant that the clergy were being regarded more definitely as sacred persons, and the laity as profane. The usual meaning, in fact, of the Greek word *laikos* is 'profane'. It had been used in earlier Christian writings to distinguish the laity from the clergy, but in those its ordinary meaning 'profane' had rather been over-ridden by its derivation from *laos*, 'people', so that it signified 'belonging to the people—the holy people—of God'. But it is interesting to find that things which *laikoi* are accepted as doing in the earlier texts, like teaching, they are forbidden to do in post-Constantinian texts. In such texts we also find, for example, that *laikoi* are forbidden to enter the sanctuary, the sacred place, now reserved for sacred persons.[6] It is natural enough for authority in a sacral society to be the privilege of sacred persons—and so it increasingly came to be in the post-Constantinian Church—especially the post-Theodosian Church. For it was Theodosius and his sons who set the seal on the Constantinian revolution.

There is a third way in which the authority of all the faithful was fatally weakened by the Constantinian revolution. The clergy, which is to say in effect the bishops, had very cogent reasons for trying to curb and if possible to eliminate any exercise of lay authority within the Church. For now that the State had become Christian, it meant that the laity included what we would call the secular authorities, from the emperor downwards. As a matter of fact, I do not know if the emperor himself was ever called 'lay'; he was certainly regarded and treated as a sacred person, and as we have seen, Eusebius called Constantine the thirteenth apostle. And during our period no churchmen, as far as I know, ever denied the right of the emperor in Constantinople to a very considerable say in Church affairs. It was the emperors who summoned councils, and even the popes, until the end of the eighth century, acknowledged that their election to their office required imperial confirmation.

Still, in resisting the idea of lay authority in the Church, which they did more persistently in the Latin West than the Greek East, churchmen were opposing the simple identification of the Church with civil society. In a society which thought of itself as Christian through and through, and which sought in the Catholic Church its sacred validation, it was only the clergy (and in a later age as we shall see, it was only the papacy) which could ensure the Church's liberty, that is to say its immunity from total subjection to the politics of the world.

And yet, in that situation, clerics and later on popes in particular found themselves unavoidably compromised. In defending the liberty of the Church from lay (that is from secular) control, they had to compromise with the world, use the methods of the world, assume many of the values, aims and prejudices of the world. There was no way out of the dilemma.

b. *The primacy of the Church of Rome*

The dilemma identified above did not become acute as far as the papacy was concerned until the high Middle Ages, which will be dealt with in our next section (AD 800–1054). In the fourth and fifth centuries, the period immediately following on Constantine's conversion, the effect of that event and its consequences on the Church of Rome was to stimulate it to a remarkably rapid and thorough elaboration of a Petrine, papal theology in opposition to what I earlier called the ideo-theology of people like Eusebius. This papal theology, which begins effectively with Pope Damasus (366–384), and reaches its complete expression with Leo the Great (440–461) was a necessary and powerful weapon to defend the genuine transcendence of the Church of God over all worldly powers and politics.

As we have seen, there is abundant evidence that from as early as AD 100 the Church of Rome had been respected by other Churches as having the pre-eminence among them. This pre-eminence was formally acknowledged by the Council of Nicaea in 325, which allotted second and third places in precedence to the Churches of Alexandria and Antioch respectively. No reasons were given; it was simply the confirmation of ancient custom. Now many people, Constantine certainly among them, will have assumed that the primacy of the Roman Church among all the Churches was simply due to its being the Church of the imperial capital. It was in virtue of such an assumption that after the capital had been transferred to Constantinople, the Council held in that city in 381 declared that the bishop of Constantinople, as 'the new Rome', should rank second after the bishop of 'old Rome' and take precedence over the bishops of Alexandria and Antioch.

The Church of Rome emphatically rejected this explanation of its primacy among the Churches. The Roman Church had been traditionally accorded this primacy because it was the Church of the apostles Peter and Paul, that is to say the place where these two apostles had been martyred, and where their remains were venerated.[7] The papal theology evolved between Popes Damasus and Leo, and most clearly expressed in the letters and sermons of the latter, elaborated this datum of tradition into the doctrine that the bishop of Rome is the successor or heir (Leo preferred this term) of Peter. Thus the primacy of the Roman Church was turned into the primacy of the bishop of that Church, though the more ancient concept did not wholly disappear. This development was in harmony with the general development of the episcopate in the first centuries.

Leo's conception of his Petrine primacy was very far-reaching; in fact little or nothing is added to it by the definition of the primacy by the first Vatican Council in the Constitution *Pastor Aeternus* in 1870. In one small respect Leo showed himself to be closer to the roots of the tradition. *Pastor Aeternus* does not refer at all to the apostle Paul in its argument; Leo, though he never calls himself the heir of Paul in the same way as he claimed to be the heir of Peter, still considers that in virtue of his office he shared Paul's 'solicitude for all the Churches' (2 Cor 11:28). He showed that solicitude in 451, when he refused to confirm canon 28 of the Council of Chalcedon. That Council, in the matter of Christological doctrine, did little more than underwrite the doctrine enunciated by Leo in his *Tome*, which he sent to the Council. But in the matter of Church order, it renewed and confirmed the canon of Constantinople, 381, giving the bishop of Constantinople the second place after the bishop of Rome. It appears that the Church of Rome had never known about the proceedings at Constantinople seventy years previously—which implies that it did not yet regard that council as an ecumenical one. In any case, Leo rejected Chalcedon's confirmation of that canon, precisely as an infringement of the ancient, and he would have said apostolic, rights of the Churches of Alexandria and Antioch.

Thus a most important consequence of the Constantinian revolution was a rapid development of the doctrine of the Petrine primacy of the popes as a defensive reaction against the Eusebian ideo-theology. The popes claimed for themselves an authority in principle entirely independent of (and ultimately superior to) the imperial or any other human authority. In claiming it for themselves, they implicitly claimed it for their colleagues the other bishops and for the whole Church. Although the claim could not always—indeed hardly ever—be made completely good in practice, it is of supreme importance that it has always stood in principle.

One point, however, has to be noticed. Although Leo, the greatest and in a sense the most typical of these fourth- and fifth-century popes, insisted that he enjoyed the fullness of authority, *plenitudo potestatis*, in the Church, received immediately from Christ in the person of Peter, it would never have occurred to him that this meant it was his duty and responsibility to *govern* the universal Church. The government of the Churches was the responsibility of the bishops, individually and in their synods. The popes, presiding over an annual synod in Rome, did exercise a fairly direct government over the Churches of central and southern Italy and the islands. And in Leo's time at least the bishop of Thessalonika was always the pope's vicar (the Middle Ages would have called him a *legatus natus*) for the supervision of the Churches of Macedonia, Greece and Illyricum. Perhaps similar arrangements obtained for the Churches of Gaul and Spain. But this kind of patriarchal authority was customary rather than Petrine, and there was never any question of trying to exercise it over the Churches of the East. Even over the Churches of the West it was not so much a controlling authority as a kind of watching brief.

c. Developments in the institution of councils

The ecclesiastical authority which was most visible to the Christian emperors from Constantine onwards was that of the bishops meeting and legislating and settling disputed questions in provincial synods or councils. They extended this institution to the convoking of general councils. The first of these to be subsequently recognised as 'ecumenical', that is to say as binding in its decisions on the whole *Catholica*, all the Churches, was the Council of Nicaea, which Constantine convoked in 325 to settle the Arian dispute that was agitating the Churches of the East.[8] But like all the later councils recognised as ecumenical before the schism between East and West, it was really a council of the Eastern Churches, with the Church of Rome represented not by its bishop in person but by a legate sent by him. The reason is that the Empire was already divided for administrative purposes into the Latin-speaking provinces of the West and the Greek-speaking provinces of the East, and it was these latter Churches in which theological disputes were most frequent and most divisive.

But as a matter of usually overlooked fact, Nicaea was not the first general council Constantine had convoked. Ten years earlier he had summoned a council of Western bishops at Arles in the south of France to pass judgement on the Donatist dispute that was tearing the African Churches apart.[9] It has never been listed as 'ecumenical', but at the beginning of the next century Augustine would refer to it as a general council.

Councils did not prove an effective instrument for exercising imperial supervision of the Church—nor indeed for the Church settling its own differences. Almost invariably, after a council, later recognised as ecumenical, had defined a disputed doctrine, the dispute raged on for decades or even centuries. Councils tended to enjoy not a contemporary but a posthumous authority. They were there for later generations to appeal to, with an acquired authority of antiquity second only to the authority of scripture itself.

But at any rate in the West, regional councils continued to be much more constructive elements in the institutional life of the Church. Councils of the African, the Spanish and the Gallican (French) Churches were of frequent, at times of routine, occurrence, and contributed to the development of the distinctive liturgies and theologies of these regions. There was in these centuries certainly no uniform Latin Church in the West, nor was such uniformity even dreamt of.

3. Developments from 800 to 1054

This is not a history of the Church, and so I will not detail the consequences for the Churches in the West of the break-up of the Roman Empire in that region from the middle of the fifth century, and the conversion of the barbarian kingdoms that occupied its territory. It meant, briefly, that while the Church was as closely entwined with secular society in the West as in the East, its position in relationship to the secular rulers was much more dominant. The power of bishops increased; they became great lords or magnates. They rarely had occasion to feel that the liberty of the Church was threatened.

The collapse of imperial power also meant that the Churches of the West became more and more isolated from those of the East. Their one link with the Christian East was in fact the Roman

Church, which throughout this period was never as exclusively and narrowly Latin as the other Western Churches. An interesting illustration is the story of the *Filioque*.[10] This word had been introduced into the Latin text of the Nicene creed, first probably in Spain and then in the Churches of England and Gaul in the course of the seventh and eighth centuries. By the time of Charlemagne, he and his bishops assumed that it had always been in the creed, and that the perfidious Greeks had deliberately left it out. So in 810 they sent a deputation to Rome to demand that the pope should condemn the Greeks for doing this. But the pope and his counsellors were better educated than the Franks, and explained to them that it was they who had introduced the word, not the Greeks who had left it out. To emphasise the Roman Church's loyalty to the text as promulgated by Nicaea and Constantinople, Pope Leo III had the text in Latin and Greek inscribed *without* the *Filioque* on silver shields, and hung up on either side of the high altar in St Peter's. It was not until two hundred years later, in 1014, that the Holy See, bowing to pressure from the German Emperor Henry II, introduced into the liturgy of the Roman Church the practice of singing the Nicene creed, with the *Filioque*, during the mass on Sundays and feast days.

For two crucial things had happened in those two hundred years. First, shortly before the pontificate of Leo III, the Holy See had taken the momentous decision to side, politically at least, with the Franks against the Byzantines; on Christmas day, 800, Leo III himself had crowned Charlemagne in Rome as emperor of the Roman Empire in the West. This was not a total repudiation of the title and dignity of the emperor in Constantinople, but it was a repudiation of his authority in Rome.[11] It was also an acknowledgement of the Holy See's dependence on a powerful secular ruler for its security. It was the beginning of a long, tortuous and stormy relationship with the dominant power in Western Europe.

The second crucial thing that happened in this period was the long degradation of the Roman Church and the Holy See from about 888 to 1049. The degradation was not total or unremitting. But for most of that time the papal throne was the plaything of powerful Roman barons. At the beginning of the tenth century there was an exceedingly influential Roman lady, Marozia, whom Gibbon described (accurately enough) as 'the mother, the mistress and the murderess of popes'. The papacy retained a symbolic prestige in the West—Rome did possess, after all, the tombs of the apostles—but exercised no power or influence over Churches elsewhere in Europe. The important point is that this did not matter to the other Churches; they were not infected or affected by the corruption of the Roman Church. New Churches were being founded in northern and north-eastern Europe; the English Church enjoyed a remarkable revival; the Byzantine Church had never been so splendid. The situation would be very different five hundred years later during the second long corruption of the Roman Church in the late fifteenth and early sixteenth centuries, as we shall see in a later chapter.

The most baleful consequence of these events was the ever increasing mutual antipathy between the Franks and the Byzantines, the Latin West and the Greek East, which was to culminate in the definitive schism of 1054. During this period the Roman Church gradually became less and less capable of performing its role of link joining the two halves of Christendom together. So when eventually the papacy was reformed on the initiative of devout and forceful German emperors, it found itself in spirit simply at the head of the Latin Churches, and vigorously inaugurated the second Christian millennium under the practical, if not theoretical, delusion that the Catholic Church and the Latin Church are one and the same thing.

NOTES

1 Lightfoot attaches this dissertation to his commentary on Philippians, because that epistle is addressed, uniquely among Paul's letters, 'to all the saints in Christ Jesus who are at Philippi, *with the bishops and deacons*'. Nowhere else does Paul so much as mention bishops and deacons. They figure prominently enough in the pastoral epistles to Timothy and Titus, which few scholars nowadays consider to have been written by Paul.

The trouble with reading a perfect classic like Lightfoot's dissertation is that it saps one of any energy to read anything else written on the subject; there seems little point. And I really do not think that either his premises or his arguments or his conclusions have been or could be faulted by later scholars and their scrutiny of the texts. His conclusions may, though, be supplemented, as by Daniélou's suggestion of another kind of ministry, mentioned below.

2 *Didachē* means 'teaching'. The full title is *The Teaching of the Twelve Apostles*. A translation by J. A. Kleist, SJ, is to be found in the *Ancient*

Christian Writers series (ACW 6; Cork, 1948). There it is described as 'an epitome of Christian morality, suited to pagan candidates for baptism', followed by a 'ritual or liturgical summary'. There is a detailed commentary on it in French by J.-P. Audet, OP (Paris, 1958).

3 Jean Daniélou and Henri Marrou, *The Christian Centuries*, vol. I: *The First Six Hundred Years* (London, 1964).

4 Thus the office of Lord High Admiral has since 1689 been exercised by 'the Lords Commissioners of the Admiralty'; and the official title of the Prime Minister is 'first Lord of the Treasury', there no longer being a Lord Treasurer, but a Commission of the Treasury.

5 An important social function of religion in most if not all societies is and has been to validate the society's conception of itself and its structures. Christianity, whether Catholic or Protestant or Orthodox, has certainly fulfilled this function in the past, and continues to fulfil it today. It is, of course, a very ambiguous function, which hardly allows for criticism of a society, its values and structures in the light of religious principles. As an example, it is clear that after the Falklands war in 1982, the British government and most of its Conservative supporters wanted a thanksgiving service that would be an exercise in civil religion, thanking God for victory, justifying the war without any reservations. The Archbishop of Canterbury and the other heads of Churches, on the other hand, considered rightly that that would be a prostitution of true Christian worship, and designed a service which enraged Mrs Thatcher and other politicians precisely because of its fidelity to the gospel for *all* nations (including the Argentinians). Christian values transcend merely social values, and the Church must always be in a position to pass judgement on civil societies, their rulers, their structures and their values.

6 See *A Patristic Greek Lexicon*, ed. G. W. H. Lampe (Oxford University Press, 1961), under *laikos*. The texts restricting the functions and rights of the laity are all post-Constantinian in date.

7 See J. M. R. Tillard, OP, *The Bishop of Rome* (Theology and Life series; Wilmington, Del., 1983).

8 Arius, a presbyter of Alexandria, was teaching that the *Logos*, the Word or the Son, is not of the same substance as the Father, that he is in fact a creature, the first of creatures. The slogan attributed to him was 'There was a time when he was not'. His great opponent was Athanasius, only a deacon at the time of Nicaea (to which he accompanied his bishop), but bishop of Alexandria from 328 to 373.

9 The Donatists were rigorists who denied that the sacraments could be validly conferred by sinners, more precisely by those who apostatised during persecution and were betrayers (*traditores*) of the sacred books. In effect, they denied the validity of the orders of the Catholic bishops, and of baptism conferred by them. Their Church duplicated the Catholic Church in North Africa, and represented a strong nationalistic sentiment.

10 The clause that says, in our Western version of the Nicene creed, that

the Holy Spirit 'proceeds from the Father *and the Son*'. The original version of the complete creed, as promulgated at the Council of Constantinople, 381, simply states that the Holy Spirit 'proceeds from the Father', quoting Jn 15:26. It was Augustine's theology that he also proceeds from the Son, and it was under his influence that the Churches of Spain first, then of England and France, introduced the phrase into the creed.

11 It so happened there was no emperor in Constantinople at the time, but an empress, Irene. She had ruled as regent for her young son Constantine VI for ten years from 780 to 790. Then a period of uneasy joint rule with him (she refused just to retire when he came of age) ended in a brief conflict, which she won in 798, securing her position as sole ruler by having him blinded.

4

THE ORDAINED MINISTRY: HIERARCHY AND PRIESTHOOD

In Chapter 1 we saw that two important concepts in the theological arsenal of the magisterial papalists are 'hierarchy' and 'priestly ministry' or sacerdotalism. These are concepts that have been grafted onto the basic dogmatic datum that the ordained ministry is one of the sacraments of the Church. Perhaps it would be even more accurate to say that they are parasitic on this datum, like mistletoe on the oak tree, not essential to the life of the main organism at all. So let us first examine the ordained ministry and the sacrament of order, and then see how these two concepts, of which we are frankly critical, are related to it.

A. The sacrament of order

That order is one of the seven sacraments of the Church is common ground between MPs and MCs, and so there is no need here to show how the definition of the Council of Trent on the subject (Decree on the sacrament of order, 15 July 1563, especially canon 3; Dz 1773) is fully consonant with the New Testament and the most ancient tradition. We shall just observe two points about the sacrament that should throw light on the essential nature of the ordained ministry.

1. One sacrament, three orders

First, though the sacrament of order is one sacrament, there are, as we know, three orders, those of deacon, presbyter/priest and bishop; and though this sacrament, like baptism and confirmation, is not repeatable, some persons in holy orders—i.e. bishops—have been ordained three times, and most of them—i.e. priests—have been ordained twice. So how is it one sacrament, and how is it not repeatable? The solution is perhaps to be found in its name, 'order'. 'Order' means 'arrangement'. So 'to ordain' means 'to arrange' or 'to set in order'. Now arranging or setting in order is something you do to things collectively. Some people are very good at arranging flowers; it would be rather odd to talk about arranging a flower. So then, when a person is ordained, whether deacon, priest or bishop, he is 'arranged', set in order. Like an isolated flower, all by himself? Surely not, but rather in relationship with other people. What other people? Other clergymen only, other ordained or arranged people? Again surely not, but in relation with all the other people we call Christians, in relation with the Church.

So I suggest that properly speaking it is not individual ordained ministers who are ordained and receive the sacrament of order, but the whole Church, whether the universal or the local Church, just as it is the whole bouquet or vase of flowers that is arranged, not just individual flowers within it. The Church is set in order, or ordained, through certain of its members being placed in certain positions within it. And because the Church itself, in its unity with Christ, is 'a kind of sacrament and instrument of the unity of mankind and the union of man with God' (*Lumen Gentium*, 1), the ordering of the Church is a sacramental act, performed by the laying-on of hands on the persons placed in those positions.

The positions vary in importance and authority, but all contribute to the essential order or sacramental structure of the Church. In that sense the orders respectively of deacon, priest and bishop are parts of the sacrament of order, parts of the sacramental ordering of the Church. But they are not parts of the sacrament in its secondary recipients, i.e. in the ordained persons. Again, ministers are ordained to their respective orders by the sacrament of laying-on of hands, and in that sense of course they receive the sacrament. But this is still only the secondary sense of ordaining or conferring the sacrament of order, though to be sure it is also the most obvious one. There is still only the one sacrament of order, through which the Church (and primarily the local Church) is set in order by the ordination of some to the order of deacons, others to the order of priests, and yet others to the order of bishops.

This affects the laity as much as the clergy, though in a different manner. For they are equally members of the Church, the community being set in order by the sacrament of order. While it is baptism/confirmation that makes Christians (sacramentally speaking) and recruits people into the Church, it is this Church, this whole people of God, this community of the baptised which is being organised, drawn up in battle array[1] so to speak, when any of its members is ordained to the office of deacon, priest or bishop.

2. Grace conferred on the Church, rather than on the individual

My second point about the sacrament of order lends further weight to my contention that it is primarily the Church or community of believers as a whole that is the recipient of the sacrament of order, and only secondarily the ordained ministers. It is that this is the only one of the seven sacraments that is not conferred on persons for their own sakes. It may, to state it in a somewhat shocking manner, be called the one sacrament that is in itself detrimental to the salvation of the individual recipient. In no way does the job of deacon or priest, let alone of bishop (and least of all of pope) assist the incumbent towards salvation. Quite the contrary. Lord Acton's dictum that all power tends to corrupt is as true of ecclesiastical as of any other power—and this has been acknowledged in the Church from the gospel itself onwards.

Of course, those ordained know that they are servants of a good and just and generous master, who does not refuse them the grace they need, and so they can be confident that the sacrament confers on them its appropriate sacramental grace. And they can therefore hope to hear one day the welcome, 'Well done, good and faithful servant; you have been faithful over little, I will set you over much; enter into the joy of your master' (Mt 25:21). But the fact remains that the rank or order to which ministers are ordained is of itself more an obstacle than an aid to its holder's salvation (and the higher the order, the truer this is). So St Augustine could say in a sermon preached on the anniversary of his ordination as bishop, 'What I am for you terrifies me; what I am with you consoles me. For you I am a bishop, but with you I am a Christian. The former is a title of duty, the latter one of grace. *The former is a danger*, the latter salvation' (my italics).[2] The text is quoted by Vatican II in *Lumen Gentium*, 32, rather curiously in its chapter on the laity, not in its chapter on 'the Hierarchical Structure of the Church, with Special Reference to the Episcopate', where it would have been more apposite.

The grace of this particular sacrament, then, is primarily a grace conferred on the Church, only secondarily on the ordained minister. In this respect it resembles those charismatic graces Paul speaks of in 1 Cor 12 and 14, which the scholastics call *gratiae gratis datae*; graces that benefit the whole body of the community without necessarily benefiting the individual member who receives them.

3. Consequences for the Church

Consequences relevant to our general theme flow from this way of envisaging the Church, and not the individual minister, as the primary recipient of the sacrament of order. The question immediately arises—What is the Church ordered or ordained *for*? We have always known what the clergy are ordained for; they are ordained for the Church. But we have not been very much in the habit of asking what the Church is for. It has been assumed to be an end in itself. Or else it has been seen as the community of salvation; so if it is for anything, it is for the salvation of its members, and the clergy are ordained to minister to the salvation of its members by being their pastors or shepherds, teaching them the true faith, providing them with the sacraments, directing them in the way they should go; for the ministry in fact of word and sacrament and government.

All this is as true as it has always been. The clergy from bishops down and deacons up are indeed ordained for the pastoral ministry of direction, of word and sacrament in the Church. But it cannot be the whole truth, because it does not really answer our question what the *Church* is ordained or set in order for. If we are satisfied with this part-answer, then we are in danger of becoming part-Christians—which the MP view of the Church of its nature tends to reduce us to. Such a part-answer or half-truth has fitted in only too well with the exaggerated individualism of the Euro-American outlook of the last two hundred years and more. Our main religious concern has been our personal salvation; the Church has been there to provide the means for it; the clergy have been there to administer the means.

This attitude has found expression too frequently in a kind of detached passivity on the part of most laypeople, whether they are devout or lax Catholics; and it has led to both laity and clergy too readily identifying the Church with the clergy, in particular with the bishops, and most particularly with the Holy See and the pope, precisely as the persons who dispose of the means of salvation which the Church is simply there (in this view) to provide. And all this in turn has fostered that high-minded (and too often high-handed) authoritarianism and paternalism on the part of ecclesiastical authorities, from parish priests upwards, which is so often part of the MP syndrome.

But now, when we consider the Church itself (*not* just the clergy) as being ordained by the sacrament of order, and ask what it is being set in order *for*, we cannot really be satisfied with the answer 'for itself and its members', any more than we have ever accepted the idea that the clergy are ordained simply for their own sake and their own good. The Church, after all, is the Church of Jesus Christ who died for all mankind and is the Saviour of the *world* (Jn 4:42). So we surely have to answer that the Church, the whole body of believers, the whole people of God, both the Church universal and the Church local, is set in order and organised *for the world*, for others who are not actually members of the Church in the most obvious sense, but are potentially so.

The Church (not just the clergy, or the bishops, or the Holy See) is the beginnings and the instrument of the kingdom of God, which Jesus Christ came to proclaim (Mk 1:14–15). The Church is the initial establishment of that kingdom (*Lumen Gentium*, 5), its bridgehead in the world, so to say. The task of the Church then is to continue the work of Christ in proclaiming the gospel of the kingdom to all creatures, and to expand the bridgehead by doing what it can to bring all mankind into the kingdom under the reign of God. The reign of God is a reign of justice and peace, of truth and love. So the Church's task is to promote justice and peace in the world, and to give an example of truth and love.

This latter task is supremely exemplified by that working for reconciliation and unity among Christians of different communions and denominations which is called the ecumenical movement. So the answer we have given, that the Church is for the world, can be developed into a threefold purpose or task: the evangelisation of unbelievers, the promotion of justice and peace, the effort to achieve reconciliation and peace among divided Christians.

The responsibilities which the Church thus has towards the 'not-Church' or the world must necessarily colour our view of the responsibilities which the Church's ordained ministers have towards the Church and its members. Their traditional responsibilities of pastoral care for the faithful by the ministry of word and sacrament and pastoral authority are still as squarely on their shoulders as they have ever been. But now these duties are given an orientation beyond their immediate object. For in this new perspective one must see the all-embracing responsibility of the clergy to be that of encouraging and enabling their fellow Christians, the whole Christian community of the Church, to meet *their* responsibilities to the 'not-Church', the world. And this simply cannot be done by 'go-and-he-goeth, come-and-he-cometh' edicts from on high. It can only be done if we recognise that the sacrament of order confers on the clergy a *ministerial*, not an imperious, authority at the service of and not over the authority shared by all the faithful; an authority which will elicit by encouragement, by respect, by consultation, by genuine and humble listening, the resources of inspiration and initiative that all the faithful can contribute to this common threefold task of the Church.[3]

B. Priesthood

The Catholic theology of ministry and order has for centuries been seriously distorted by an exaggerated and indeed almost exclusive concentration on the concept of priesthood. For my questioning of this concept my MP critics will be able to quote against me the same decree of the Council of Trent which I referred to at the beginning of this chapter in support of the doctrine that order is one of the seven sacraments (see chapter 1 and canon 1 of that decree: Dz 1764 and 1771). But I am not suggesting that the concept should be dropped altogether from our doctrine on order and ministry; I am only proposing that it should be politely transferred to a back seat. That Trent, following a pretty long tradition, put it in the driving seat is not a point, in my submission, on which we are bound to follow the Council.

1. Use of 'priest', 'priesthood'

a. *In the New Testament*

The fact is (a fact which both pre- and post-Tridentine theology, and MP theology to this day have blandly ignored) the concept of priesthood is never applied in the New Testament to the ordained ministry. It is applied in Hebrews to Jesus Christ. In the proper and unqualified sense of the term it is applicable to him alone, the one and only high-priest of our confession, a priest for ever according to the order of Melchizedek, whose priesthood supersedes once and for all the Old Testament priesthood of the sons of Aaron. Next it is applied, by participation or communion in Christ, to all believers in 1 Pet 2:5, 9 and Rev 1:6; 5:10. We are all 'a kingdom of priests to our God' (these New Testament texts are roughly quoting Ex 19:6) in so far as we share in Christ's priestly role and sacrifice. We share in this priesthood in virtue of our faith and our baptism. St Thomas teaches (and he was not being original) that sacramental character, in particular the baptismal character, is a participation in the priesthood of Christ.[4] But nowhere in the New Testament where bishops or presbyters or deacons are mentioned are they referred to as priests, or in sacerdotal terms, or as having special sacerdotal functions.

Why then, you may ask, do we talk about the three orders of bishop, *priest*, and deacon? It is because here the word 'priest' is just the English form of the Greek word *presbyteros*, which means 'elder', just as 'bishop' is the English form of *episkopos*, meaning 'supervisor', and 'deacon' is the English form of *diakonos*, meaning 'servant' or 'waiter'. Now when I tell you that 'bishop' basically means 'supervisor' and 'deacon' basically means 'servant', you do not have any difficulty, I suppose, in accepting what I say. But when I tell you that 'priest' basically means 'elder', you will probably put up a stiff resistance; and quite rightly, because you know perfectly well it means nothing of the kind. It means a person with sacred powers and duties, especially the power and duty of offering sacrifice to God—or to the gods, because we are all familiar with the existence of pagan priests as well as Christian and Israelite priests, whereas we rarely if ever talk of pagan bishops and deacons.

And yet the truth is that the English word 'priest' is a short form, produced by stammering and illiterate Anglo-Saxon tongues, of the Greek *presbyteros*, or rather of the Latin form of it, *presbyter*, which equally certainly mean 'elder'. The Latin and Greek respectively for what we now nearly always mean by 'priest' are *sacerdos* and *hiereus*; and the word 'priest' is correctly used in English translations of the Bible for these words, and for the Hebrew equivalent, *kohen*. And the point is, to repeat, that in the New Testament the people called *presbyteri* (priests) and the people called *episcopi* (bishops) and the people called *diaconi* (deacons) are never called *sacerdotes* or *hiereis* (priests). Absolutely never. Not a single time. This is the point that Trent and the MP theology totally ignore.

How then did the word 'priest', which started life as equivalent to *presbyter* (elder), come to mean something quite different, namely *sacerdos* (priest)? It's a long, long story.

In the New Testament, as we saw in Chapter 2, section C.1, *episcopus* and *presbyter* are just two names for the same officer, one designating function, the other status. But by the middle of the second century they had become distinguished in the way we have been familiar with ever since, and each local Church was governed by a bishop, assisted by his presbyters and deacons. Each local Church, moreover, was about the size of an average modern parish, which could assemble all together to celebrate the eucharist on the Lord's day. So it was the bishop who normally presided at the celebration of the eucharist.

Now from very early on the eucharist had come to be talked of in sacrificial terms as the sacrifice through which Christians participate in the one and only perfect sacrifice of Jesus Christ. Indeed the New Testament accounts of the institution of the eucharist already employ sacrificial language. The oldest Christian document outside the New Testament, the *Didache*,[5] says of the eucharist (sec. 14)

> . . . your sacrifice must not be defiled. For here we have the saying of the Lord, In every place and time offer me a pure sacrifice; for I am a mighty king, says the Lord, and my name spreads terror among the nations (Mal 1:11, 14).

b. Subsequent development

So by the beginning of the third century at least, and probably earlier, we find bishops, as the officiating dignitaries at the Christian sacrifice, referred to as *sacerdotes*, i.e. 'priests'; bishops, but not yet presbyters. Indeed, wherever the word *sacerdos* occurs in ancient Christian texts in a ministerial context, right up to the sixth or seventh centuries, it should not be translated as 'priest', since as it always refers to bishops that would give a misleading impression. 'High priest' would be the most just rendering. I presume the same is true of *hiereus* in Greek texts.

But when from the seventh century onwards the gospel was carried deep into the barbarian nations of northern Europe which had never been part of the Roman Empire, beginning with Patrick's mission to Ireland and Gregory the Great's mission to the Anglo-Saxons, bishops were few and far between. They may have done the initial evangelising, like Augustine of Canterbury in England and Boniface in Germany over a century later. But as the Church came to be established in these countries it was organised into huge dioceses, which no longer corresponded in the least to a modern parish. So the *usual* officiant at mass whom people were familiar with was no longer a bishop but a presbyter. They couldn't pronounce him properly, so they shortened him to 'priest'—and thought of him as a *sacerdos* because he was offering the holy sacrifice among them. And so 'priest' came to mean primarily *sacerdos* and, cuckoo-like, pushed whatever word of Germanic origin the Saxons had used for such sacred officials entirely out of circulation.

2. Distortions of the notion of 'priesthood'

As I said at the beginning of this section, I have no intention of casting doubt upon the essential propriety of the theological development by which the Christian ministry has come to be so closely associated with the concept of priesthood. Order is a sacrament; the eucharist is the heart of the sacramental system, indeed the heart of the Church and the focus of its life and task; ministers are ordained to serve the Church; and so to see their service focused primarily on the eucharist is valid and proper.

But a practically exclusive emphasis on the priestly nature of the ordained ministry, a view of it as instituted quite simply for the celebration of the eucharistic sacrifice, has a very distorting effect on our notion of Church and Christian life and responsibilities, and seriously limits our capacity for adaptation. Let us examine three such distortions.

a. Sacralising clergy, desacralising laity

The first distortion is that it sacralises the clergy, so that we talk about holy orders and the sacred ministry, and thus desacralises the laity who are not thought of as officially holy or sacred any more. But of course, they are; they are the *plebs sancta* of the old Canon of the mass. The great sacrament of consecration or hallowing is baptism, not order. But we touched on this unfortunate phenomenon of the sacralisation of the ministry in Chapter 3, section B.1 and 2, and so need say no more about it here. Except perhaps to say that in our present thoroughly secularised age it has assisted the relegation of the Christian religion to its own little optional Sunday corner—and the sacred clergy with it. Hence, partly, the feeling of irrelevance that afflicts many priests, and hence too, perhaps, much of the so-called crisis of vocations. It still, too, seems to be official Vatican policy, though it is hardly working in practice, to leave the 'secular' part of the Church's mission to the world, the promotion of peace and justice, to the laity, and to confine the clergy (with the exception, perhaps, of the pope) to the more sacred spheres of pastoral ministry and evangelisation, in which the laity are not encouraged to meddle.

b. The nature of 'ministry'

The envisaging of the Christian ministry simply as a priesthood has inhibited in Catholic theological circles any profound reflection on the priesthood of all believers, which was allowed at the Reformation to become a Protestant war cry.[6] More destructively, perhaps, it has inhibited any profound reflection on the priesthood of ordained ministers, because the assumption has long been that this is a priesthood in the strict and unqualified sense, just like the Old Testament priesthood of the sons of Aaron. Indeed, at the time when Christian presbyters were beginning to be thought of simply as priests, the Christian ministry was being assiduously assimilated by Frankish theologians to the levitical priesthood of the Old Testament in far too rigid and oversimplified a manner. The Catholic Church was in fact extensively 'Judaised' by these theologians, with the Emperor Charlemagne as their patron, and this has had lasting and anti-evangelical effects.

But what is the *true* nature of the Christian ministerial priesthood? It can only be grasped in relationship on the one hand with the priesthood of Christ himself, which is the one and only priesthood in the full, strict meaning of the word; and on the other hand with the primary and basic participation in Christ's priesthood, which is that of the whole Church and all its members, conferred by the sacraments of baptism and confirmation—the priesthood of all believers. The ministerial priesthood, then, is a secondary participation in Christ's proper priesthood, a participation which does not make the ordained minister more of a priest, more strictly and properly a priest than the baptised lay person (*Lumen Gentium*, 10), but which is another kind of participation in Christ's proper priesthood, a participation for service.

I suggest that it is the essential function of ministers as *priests* (but I am not to be taken as *defining* ministers as priests) to represent and 'activate' or 'enable' the priestly, sacerdotal power of the community of the faithful as a whole. It is the community as a whole, not just the bishop or presbyter, which properly offers the sacrifice of the mass; that is to say, sacramentally participates in the sacrifice of Christ. But it needs to be enabled (or 'set in order') to do this by the sacramentally representative action of the sacramentally ordained minister.

It is still very common—at least in Lesotho and Southern Africa generally—to see on so many ordination cards the text 'A priest for ever according to the order of Melchizedek', and certainly to hear that refrain and verses from Psalm 110 sung during the ordination ceremony, while the newly ordained priest's hands are being anointed. But this is an improper use of the text. It is applicable properly in the New Testament dispensation *only* to Jesus Christ. If it may be applied by participation, improperly but legitimately, to the ordained presbyter, *a fortiori* it can be applied with equal legitimacy and no more improperly to any baptised Christian.

c. Over-emphasis on presbyters

Within the ranks of the ordained ministry itself, the concentration on the notion of priesthood and its immediate association with presbyters have meant that it is the second rank of ordained ministers which has received all the theological attention and been regarded as absolutely essential. Bishops have been seen just as 'high priests', the ones with authority over the others, and it has been felt to be normal to have comparatively few of them, and often with vast dioceses. As for deacons, since they are no use for the essential priestly work of saying mass or hearing confessions, to all intents and purposes they have ceased to exist in the last thousand years of Church history, until Vatican II. Certainly during this period they have not played any meaningful role in Church life, whereas in the first ten centuries they were very important people in the Church, often more so than the presbyters, to the intense annoyance of that irascible presbyter or priest St Jerome.[7] Nowadays we are trying to revive the ministry of deacons, to make sense of it. But I do not see how we can succeed if we continue to consider the essence of the ordained ministry to be found in the concept of priesthood.

In actual theological fact priests (i.e. presbyters, ordained ministers of the second rank) are not the absolutely indispensable order, any more than deacons are. As the Church has got along comfortably enough with next to no deacons for the last thousand years, so it could manage well enough for the next thousand with next to no priests (presbyters)—*provided* it continued to have bishops. That is the absolutely indispensable order. This, I suggest, is meant by its being said in *Lumen Gentium*, 21 that 'by episcopal consecration is conferred the fullness of the sacrament of order'.

But how, you may ask, could they manage without priests to assist them in their pastoral work? They could manage very well—if we returned to the pattern or structure of the early Church where every community of Christians, almost, had its bishop, however small it was. Suppose—and there is nothing theologically impossible in this—that every parish priest were to be ordained bishop, and every parish declared a diocese or local Church; you would then at least see that priests (presbyters) are useful and convenient, but not absolutely necessary.

We have seen that in the New Testament bishops and presbyters were not distinguished from each other, being only two names for the same functionaries. At the Reformation the Presbyterian Reformers (Calvinists) made the mistake of assuming that this meant that in the apostolic Church there were no bishops in the later sense, and therefore they abolished the office of bishop. But what it really meant was that in the apostolic Church there were no presbyters/priests in the later sense; there were only two orders, those of bishop and deacon, as Paul mentions them in Phil 1:1.

I am not proposing this as a desirable reform of Church structure at the present time—though I think it may have definite advantages. I merely mention it to show how flexible the sacrament of order is, and how we would do well to release it from the rigid concepts of priesthood and hierarchy (see next section), so that we may then have theological room to modify the structures of the Church, that is to say, principally of the ordained ministry. We need to do this in order to meet the requirements of the Church in the modern world—and the requirements of the modern world through the Church. We need to be free and able to do it, in order to meet the ecumenical commitment which the Church of Vatican II has taken upon itself at the prompting of the Holy Spirit.

C. Hierarchy

Coming now to the concept of hierarchy, we can say that it gathers up and concentrates upon the Church's structures of authority all those overtones and connotations of the concept of priesthood which we have just been scrutinising. Like priesthood it is a concept that now has rights of citizenship in the republic of Catholic theological ideas, being employed in the decree of Trent we have already referred to, canon 6 (Dz 1776)—'If anyone says that in the Catholic Church there is not a hierarchy, instituted by divine ordination, which consists of bishops, presbyters and ministers, let him be anathema'—and again, though without the anathema, in Vatican II's constitution *Lumen Gentium* in the title of chapter 3, 'On the hierarchical constitution of the Church . . .'; and in sec. 20 of this chapter the Church is called 'a hierarchically ordered society'.

So I am not suggesting that we forgo the concept altogether. But as with priesthood, as long as it is over-emphasised and its connotations remain part of the uncriticised, unexamined furniture of the Catholic mind, it makes it all that more difficult for the Church's ordained ministers, from the pope downwards, to make the adaptations of style and structure that we of the MC school are arguing to be urgently needed.

We begin our examination of the concept, then, by noting that it is not a New Testament term. This of course does not bar its theological or dogmatic use. The same is the case with 'consubstantial', for example, in trinitarian dogma, or 'person' and 'nature' in Christological language. But it does mean that the term needs to justify itself, and has no right to be taken for granted as a concept of Christian doctrine. About 'hierarchy' we can further remark that besides not being a New Testament term, it is *prima facie* discordant with such unambiguously New Testament concepts as ministry or service, and brotherhood.

Its original Greek meaning of control or management of sacred things is not necessarily contrary to those concepts, though it is rather remote from central New Testament concerns and points of view. But by the time it came to be introduced into Christian terminology, largely by Pseudo-Dionysius[8] about AD 500, it had become a term of Neoplatonic mysticism, to signify the strictly graded order of being in the Neoplatonic view of things. There is the celestial hierarchy of angels in their serried ranks, and corresponding to it or reflecting it on earth there is the ecclesiastical hierarchy of sacred ministers in theirs. It practically signifies a cosmic caste system; and from there comes the most common, and to my mind the most objectionable overtone of the word today: a hierarchical society normally means one in which rigid distinctions of status are all-important, are indeed constitutive of the society. *This* is what is discordant with New Testament concepts of service and brotherhood.

Then again, Pseudo-Dionysius' hierarchies meant a chain of being from highest (God) to lowest, a chain in which being, blessings and goodness were mediated to the lower by the higher. The higher a being in the hierarchical scale, the closer it is to God, the more godlike. Lower beings only participate in the divine influence through the mediation of the higher. Whether or no this is more or less the case among the hosts of heaven does not concern us here. Such was the authority of these writings, until the Renaissance proved them to be pious forgeries, that all mediaeval theologians from Gregory the Great to Thomas Aquinas and beyond were convinced that it was. But that this celestial hierarchy should be regarded as a kind of model of the ecclesiastical hierarchy, and be applied in all seriousness to the human society of the Church, concerns us very much as a grave distortion of what the Church is.

For the inescapable conclusion is that the higher a man is in the ecclesiastical hierarchy the closer he is to God, and that his function is to mediate the grace of God to those lower down the scale. The man highest in the ecclesiastical hierarchy is the pope, and he —on this view—is so close to God that in some MP popular devotion and MP curial etiquette he has almost become identified with God, and given titles that most properly belong to God alone, like 'Holy Father' and 'the Most Holy'.[9] This, of course, is not genuine Christianity, it is religious mythology bolstering a particular ecclesiastical ideology. It is rightly stigmatised by Protestants as 'popery' and by good and upright Catholics as 'papolatry'. Nor is it just the pope but the whole hierarchy of bishops, and in the common consciousness most immediately perhaps the priests, who are seen as intermediaries between God and the ordinary lay believer, so that without their sacred ministrations the grace of Christ cannot reach him.

This may not be the formal teaching of the MP ultramontanes, but it is the inference from much of their practice, an inference which is supported by exaggerated stress on the unexamined concept of hierarchy. And it is a most serious distortion of the twin principles of the New Testament, which are central to a true idea of the Church, that Christ is the *sole* mediator between God and mankind (1 Tim 2:5; cf. Acts 4:12), and that he identifies himself with all who believe in him and are gathered together in his name (Mt 18:20), but above all with the least of his brethren (Mt 25:40, 45). So it is the poor and the little ones who are closest to God, not hierarchs as such.

Perhaps a word or two more needs to be said about mediation. Christ does share his role of mediator with the Church as he shares all his roles or titles, like Christ, King, Priest and Prophet —and Son and Servant. But he shares it with *all* believers, not just with ordained ministers, and on a principle of identification or communion, not on a principle of Platonic, hierarchical participation. The most obvious sharers in his mediation are the saints in heaven, supremely the blessed Virgin Mary. That is why we ask them for their prayers. The manner of mediating is by intercession and self-sacrifice as it was with Christ himself, not by the exercise of a sacred office. All Christians therefore can mediate for others *in* Christ, not in addition to Christ; lay people for clergymen quite as much as clergymen for lay people. This is the communion of saints. This is what we express our faith in after expressing it in the holy catholic Church, according to the Apostles' creed—not in the hierarchy of saints.

NOTES

1 Cf. Song of Songs 6:10, according to the Latin Vulgate: 'terrible as an army in battle array'. RSV has 'terrible as an army with banners'. The charms of the bride, of course, are being described, and she is a figure of the Church.

2 *Sermon* 340: PL 38, 1483. See also his *Letter* 21 (PL 33, 88), which he wrote to his bishop Valerius just after he had been ordained priest very much against his will and quite unexpectedly. He asks for a short leave of absence in order to prepare himself for his new responsibilities, and says:

> I beg you to reflect, in your religious wisdom, that in this life, and especially in this age, there is nothing easier and more pleasant and agreeable to men than the office of bishop or priest or deacon if it is undertaken in a perfunctory way as a matter of respectability—and nothing in God's eyes sadder, more wretched and damnable. Again, nothing in this life, and especially in this age is harder, more

toilsome and dangerous than the office of bishop or priest or deacon; but in God's eyes nothing more blessed if one soldiers on in the way our commander-in-chief bids us.

3 It is in the light of such considerations as these that all the current questions about the ministry should be discussed. Can the Church's ordained ministers provide the necessary leadership and encouragement in these tasks if they do not include women in their ranks, if they do not include married people in their ranks, if some of them do not engage in various kinds of secular work not obviously ministerial, if they are only selected and trained in the traditional way by minor and major seminaries? These are questions which the MP ultramontanes in the seats of power refuse to allow to be officially discussed. They have not learned the lesson of King Canute.

4 *Summa Theologiae* IIIa, 63, 3.

5 See Chapter 3, note 2.

6 Vatican II has restored this New Testament concept to a proper position of honour in Catholic teaching. See especially *Lumen Gentium*, 10 and 11. But the document offers a very inadequate paragraph (the second half of *Lumen Gentium*, 10) on the relationship between the priesthood of all believers and the ministerial faithful, without explicitly referring either of them to the priesthood of Christ. The concept has yet to filter down into everyday Catholic catechetical teaching, and is studiously ignored by MPs.

7 St Jerome (*c.* 340–420) was for the first part of his ecclesiastical career secretary to Pope Damasus. He did not really relish the way it was rather more often deacons than presbyters who were elected bishops in those days. So he had a fair-sized chip on his shoulder about bishops pulling rank on priests. He would entirely have endorsed Bishop Lightfoot's theory that at the beginning bishops were no more than jumped-up presbyters, and not localised apostles.

8 An unknown writer, possibly a Syrian monk (possibly even a supporter of the Monophysite heresy), who composed his works on *The Celestial Hierarchy*, *The Ecclesiastical Hierarchy* and *The Divine Names* and then attributed them to Dionysius the Areopagite, Paul's Athenian convert (Acts 17:34). This immediately gave them an authority of the most incontestable weight—people were very easily taken in by forgeries in those days before history as a science was a practical proposition, there being few books and fewer libraries.

9 At the height of the ultramontane fervour in the 1860s that led up to the definition of papal primacy and infallibility in 1870 at Vatican I, Louis Veuillot, the editor of the French ultramontane paper *L'Univers*, was publishing hymns in honour of Pius IX that any ordinary sensibility would consider blasphemous. Thus there is a hymn of the breviary for the office of sext that begins *Rerum Deus tenax vigor*—'O God, the strength and stay of all creation'; Veuillot emended it to *Rerum Pius tenax*

vigor. No rebuke is recorded as having been administered by the Holy Office, or any other agency of the Holy See.

Patriarch Maximus IV Saigh of Antioch, whom we shall meet in Chapter 8 below at Vatican II, expressed himself deeply shocked—and rightly so—at finding the following expressions in an Italian book 'placed in all hands'—in fact *Meditazioni* attributed to Don Bosco:

> The Pope is God on earth . . . Jesus has placed the Pope above the Prophets, above the Precursor, above the Angels; Jesus has set the Pope on the very level of God.

That a book containing such sentiments, which are not just exaggerations of popular devotion, but are scandalously and blasphemously false, should receive the *imprimatur*, and never be censured, is indeed disturbing. The truth, as the patriarch pointed out, is that Jesus confided the primatial 'jurisdiction to Peter—a man like all other human beings, a repentant sinner'; see Acts 10:26 (AS I, iv, p. 295).

5

AUTHORITY IN THE CHURCH IN THE SECOND MILLENNIUM

In Chapter 3 we considered developments in the authority structures of the Church during the first millennium at various levels—popular, episcopal and papal. In this chapter, dealing with the second millennium, our attention will be confined to the development of papal authority, which overshadows all the rest. The development begins—in historical perspective, at a gallop—almost simultaneously with the definitive schism between the Latin Churches of the West and the Greek Churches of the East in 1054. This coincidence of these two events is not fortuitous. So we must begin by reflecting on the importance, for our subject, of the schism.

A. The significance and consequences of the schism of 1054

To be sure, when the schism occurred, with the papal legate Cardinal Humbert excommunicating the patriarch of Constantinople, Michael Caerularius, and the latter replying in kind, no one knew it was going to be permanent.[1] There had been several breaches before between Rome and Constantinople. Nonetheless, it *was* permanent, and as the years wore on without its being mended, the Latins of the West, who were experiencing a vigorous intellectual renaissance, grew accustomed to thinking of the Greeks as 'outside the Church'. Consequently they grew into the habit of identifying the Catholic Church, practically if not theoretically speaking, with the Latin Church or Churches. It is a habit that Latin Christians in Rome and the rest of the world have not yet grown out of.

This means that the Church of Rome and the other Latin Churches of the West no longer had any real or imaginative experience of the majority of the Churches of the *Catholica* (the Greek and oriental Churches) being Churches over which the papal primacy was scarcely exercised at all, though its existence was acknowledged. Consequently they began to identify or confuse (and still do) the pope's divinely bestowed Petrine authority and primacy within the whole Catholic Church, and his purely customary and canonical authority over the Latin Churches as 'patriarch of the West'.

In other words, we can say that the schism of 1054 took the brake off the inflated extension and exaltation of papal authority, which has dominated the institutional history of the Catholic (Latin) Church from that day to this. This process has taken slightly different forms in three main periods, the mediaeval (1054–1564), the post-Tridentine (1564–1870), and the modern (1870–1962). Let us examine each period in turn.

B. Development of papal authority, 1054–1564

It was in the mediaeval period that the papal claims were the most inflated, e.g. in pronouncements of Gregory VII (1073–1085) and Boniface VIII (1294–1303),[2] claims of a universal and absolute sovereignty over all other authorities, secular as well as ecclesiastical; claims in virtue of which, for example, Alexander VI (1492–1503) divided the whole world, not yet under the jurisdiction of Christian sovereigns, between the monarchs of Spain and Portugal in 1493.

These claims, like a great deal of mediaeval political and legal theory, were hardly realistic, and the attempts to put them into practice involved the papacy in continuous wrangles and wars with secular rulers. The chief motive behind the so-called Hildebrandine reforms (see below, note 2), launched by Gregory VII and his immediate predecessors, was to free and preserve the Church from the control of lay princes. In principle, to begin with, the popes were demanding that the princes should respect the traditional canonical rights of election to bishoprics and abbacies that belonged to cathedral chapters and monastic communities. But the princes, of course, resisted. Hence the so-called wars of investiture[3] between papacy and empire, and related conflicts above all with the kings of England and France.

The net result of this endless skirmishing, by the time we get to the fourteenth century, was not the restoration of the canonical rights of election, but practical arrangements between the papal curia and secular rulers to share appointments to high ecclesiastical offices between them—the pope would agree to the king's man being appointed to York, for example, if the king would agree to the pope's man getting Canterbury. The losers were the bishops, and episcopal authority, which was not delivered from royal control, and at the same time lost more and more ground to papal regulation.

In addition to this, the increasing centralisation of administrative authority in the Roman curia led eventually to ever deepening ecclesiastical corruption. For the first 150 years or so after the Hildebrandine reforms began, the Holy See was indeed the driving force behind the reform of the Church, and this culminated in the great pontificate of Innocent III (1198–1216), and the fourth Lateran Council of 1216. But the administrative machine that was built up bit by bit in the twelfth century needed financing; the easiest, perhaps the only way of raising the necessary funds was by turning the papal jurisdiction over other local Churches into a source of income, for example by the system of 'provision'[4] to lucrative benefices of officials of the curia. They would thus be paid for their curial services by drawing the income from a benefice (e.g. a canonry or deanery—or even a bishopric) in England, France, Scotland, or Castile which they never visited and where the pastoral duties involved were performed, if at all, by some poorly paid 'vicar'.

It was against this kind of abuse that the great bishop of Lincoln in the thirteenth century, Robert Grosseteste, protested 'Obediently I disobey'. The visible symptoms of this institutional corruption of the papacy, and consequently, through its grip on the central power ganglions, of the whole Latin Church, were in turn the Avignon period of almost seventy years (an ominous number), ending in 1377;[5] the great schism, lasting forty years (another ominous number) from 1377 to 1417, during which there were never less than two and sometimes three rival popes; and finally the scandalous worldliness of the Renaissance popes from 1471 (Sixtus IV) to 1521 (Leo X).

The expansion of papal authority in these centuries did not occur without ecclesiastical and theological opposition. The kind exemplified by Grosseteste's protest was that of conservative churchmen who still cherished the relative autonomy of local Churches and the autonomous authority of the bishops. But by the time of the great schism this kind of opposition had been overtaken by what is known as the conciliarist movement, whose leading figures were theologians in the university of Paris. They proposed what may loosely be called a parliamentary (conciliar) form of government for the universal (Latin) Church. For them as for their papalist adversaries the primary reference of the word 'Church' was no longer to the local Church, but to the universal Church, increasingly identified in these centuries with the Roman Church. The conciliarists dominated the Council of Constance (1414–1418), which succeeded in putting an end to the great schism and legislated for regular and frequent general councils, to which the pope and the papal curia would be responsible. The scheme was, for many reasons, even more unrealistic than the pretensions of the papal absolutism it sought to control, and it broke down within a few years.

The next serious opposition to papalist claims and practices came with the Protestant Reformation, which simply rejected them altogether and established new forms of ecclesiastical organisation (or variations of old ones), which it is not in our brief to discuss here. From the Catholic point of view, the Protestant Reformation led to the Council of Trent and the Counter-Reformation. What is at first sight rather strange is that the conciliar decrees, which were designed to define Catholic doctrine where it had been called in question by the Protestants on a great number of points from justification to the sacraments, nowhere touch on the matter of papal authority, which the Protestants were certainly repudiating. The nearest I can find to a conciliar statement on the subject is canon 8 of the decree on the sacrament of order (15 July 1563): 'If anyone says that bishops, who are appointed[6] by the authority of the Roman pontiff, are not legitimate and true bishops, but a human invention: let him be anathema' (Dz 1778).

The reason, however, is not far to seek. The bishops at the Council would have found it very hard to agree on a definition. The Spanish bishops, whose sovereign was the Emperor Charles V, were a very powerful block there, and neither they nor the emperor (nor the king of France and his bishops, for that matter) were enthusiastic papalists. But it is perhaps worthy of note that they could not even bring themselves to re-affirm the teaching of the Council of Florence on the subject, in the bull of union with the Greeks, *Laetentur Caeli*, of 6 July 1439 (Dz 1307). But neither, rather sadly, was anyone in Rome or at Trent moved by the cataclysm of the Reformation to rethink traditional mediaeval attitudes on the subject.

C. Papal authority, 1564–1870

What the Counter-Reformation produced at the end of the sixteenth century was a radically reformed and reorganised curia (the
present structure of Roman congregations dates from this
period). This, and the practical limitation to the ecclesiastical
sphere of papal claims to universal authority (Pius v's ill-starred
excommunication and deposition of Elizabeth I of England notwithstanding), tended in themselves to make papal control of the
whole of Church life and of local Churches and missionary ven-
tures much more effective than it had ever been in the Middle
Ages.

But on the other hand the papal absolutism was checked by a far
more powerful opposition than the mediaeval conciliarist movement. We have just observed that Charles v would not tolerate
any very close papal grip on the Church in his dominions. Well,
the same would be true of the other absolute monarchs of post-
Renaissance Europe, above all of the French kings from the
seventeenth century onwards. It was from them and their court
theologians that the opposition to papalism acquired the name of
Gallicanism. Gallicanism had a very high notion of the identity
and rights of the local Church, but now in the sense of the national
Church—in particular of the Church of France. It could be dubbed the Catholic version of the Anglicanism of Henry VIII and
Elizabeth—a national Church effectively controlled by the
monarchy, but still in communion (not always very friendly)
with the Roman Church. So in fact the rights and privileges of the
French Church, the *Ecclesia gallicana*, meant the rights of the king
of France over that Church.

In this assertion of royal rights over national Churches the
Habsburgs did not lag behind the Bourbons, and in the
eighteenth century variants on the theme of Gallicanism arose in
Germany and Austria known as Febronianism and Josephism.
The idea was the same in all cases: severely to restrict the applica-
tion of papal authority in these territories. It was a contest between a papal absolutism (or pretension to it) on the one hand and
royal absolutisms on the other. Thus the Gallican opposition to
extreme papalism was even more compromised by its political
motivations than conciliarism had been. But in any case, Gallicanism received its death wound with the French Revolution,
and though it still had its following in the nineteenth century, it
was given the *coup de grâce* by the first Vatican Council and its

constitution *Pastor Aeternus* on papal primacy and infallibility in 1870.

D. Papal authority, 1870–1962

What made the 1870 definition possible was the advance of secularism and the secular state in the nineteenth century. It is not that the days of absolute monarchies were now over—we call them dictatorships nowadays. But for the most part they are no longer as interested in religion as they used to be, and provided the Church 'sticks to the sacristy', it may, as far as they are concerned, organise itself how it wishes. This is, I grant, an oversimplification, and there have been several Church–State conflicts since 1870, quite apart from the unceasing struggle between the Church and communism. But it states the trend; and in any case, communist states are not concerned to control the Church and religion, but to encourage them to wither away altogether. It is, as they say, quite a different ball game, more like that of the first centuries between the Church and the pagan Roman Empire— and perhaps requiring in the Church radically new strategies and organisation.

In any case, from 1870 on, extreme papalism (though not actually underwritten dogmatically by the 1870 definitions) held the field unopposed within the Catholic Church until the assembly of the second Vatican Council of 1962. Since the nineteenth century this extreme papalism has been known as ultramontanism, and we are calling it magisterial papalism. To all intents and purposes it identifies the Church with the papacy; 'the Church says', 'the Church teaches' and similar phrases in sermons, pastorals, encyclicals and catechisms are heard (and uttered) as meaning 'the pope says', 'the pope teaches'.

Now that the entirely secular states of the modern world were no longer interested in running the Church, the papacy had a free hand in controlling, very tightly indeed, all appointments and activities in the local Churches that constitute the Latin Church throughout the world. Right up to the publication of the Code of Canon Law in 1917 the direct appointment of bishops by the Holy See ('provision' to bishoprics and other benefices such as we saw being exercised in the Middle Ages) was not the normal canonical procedure. The official canonical norm was still election of bishops by deans and chapters, the most common practice was their nomination by governments. But after 1917, and even more

so after the latest revision of canon law in 1984, papal appointment has been treated as the *normal* canonical procedure. Centralisation of power in the Church proceeds relentlessly on its way.

As a result the very concept of the local Church had virtually
disappeared, until it began to revive with the new perspectives of
Vatican II. It was replaced by the concept of 'diocese', a term that
had certainly long been in use, a purely administrative term
borrowed from the late Roman Empire. It means little more than
'district'. Most Catholics therefore, a great many priests and
religious, and probably most bishops have come to think of their
dioceses simply as administrative districts of the universal Catholic Church, and of the bishops themselves as no more than the
pope's delegates, agents, representatives or vicars in their respective dioceses. I doubt if this common way of thinking has been
much altered by the second Vatican Council expressly stating that
it is erroneous (*Lumen Gentium*, 27). That the Council thought it
necessary to repudiate this manifest error shows how far ultramontanism, or magisterial papalism, has succeeded in infecting
the modern Catholic (Latin) mind.

This very brief survey of the last millennium shows at least this:
that magisterial papalism is the product of this millennium and
not an institution of the gospel. It is the product of highly complex, often thoroughly perplexing, historical circumstances. It
began as a vigorous movement of Church reform and Church
liberty from secular political control. It has proved rather more
often to be an obstacle to Church reform, and has not infrequently
seriously compromised the Church's freedom from manipulation
by powerful political and socio-economic interests.[7] But in any
case, whether it has been a development for good or ill (I think it
has been both), it is clearly not a doctrinally *necessary* development. My suggestion in this book is that development in this area
in the coming millennium is going to be, and ought to be, on the
lines of ministerial collegialism.

To substantiate this further I must first attack the key MP
notion of *magisterium* (a very recent growth, compared with
hierarchy and priesthood), and then offer a critical comparison
between Vatican I's *Pastor Aeternus* and Vatican II's *Lumen Gentium*. Then, this should equip us to conclude with a utopian sketch
of the Church's authority structures as I think they ought to be
and hope they will become in the first century of the third millennium.

NOTES

1 Since Pope Paul VI met Patriarch Athenagoras I shortly after Vatican II, and they exchanged documents rescinding this ancient mutual excommunication, the question may seriously be asked whether the schism still exists. If an excommunication is rescinded it means communion is restored. Now it is true that that splendid gesture of good will (of the sort which Paul VI was peculiarly good at) has not been interpreted by either the Catholic or the Orthodox establishment as restoring full communion. But what it ought to have done, and what I maintain we can insist it has done, notwithstanding any poses and postures to the contrary, is demonstrate that in the mind *and the practice* of the Holy See the centuries of identifying the Catholic Church with the Latin Church are over and done with.

2 Before his election as Gregory VII, Cardinal Hildebrand had been the leading spirit in the new movement for reform, which is often therefore known as the Hildebrandine reform, though the expression 'Gregorian reform' is also used. Shortly after his election he drew up a famous document called the *Dictatus Papae*. David Knowles in *The Christian Centuries*, vol. 2: *The Middle Ages* (London, 1969), p. 175, calls it 'a logical translation into practice of the unlimited commission of Christ to Peter . . . which if put into execution would show a command of power and a degree of centralisation never exercised or contemplated hitherto'. One of its statements is to the effect that the pope, in virtue of his office, is automatically *sanctus*, a saint.

Boniface VIII succeeded to the papacy after its real power had passed its apogee, a fact which he was, however, unwilling to accept. So he engaged in a political duel to the death with the king of France, Philip IV the Fair. The pope lost, was captured by a henchman of the king's at Anagni and died soon after. Meanwhile, about a year before (18 November 1302), he had published the bull *Unam Sanctam* which as Knowles says (*op. cit.*, p. 336) 'has been regarded as the *ne plus ultra* of the claims of the mediaeval papacy'. 'There can be little doubt', he goes on, 'that Boniface himself meant it to be an assertion of the paramountcy, if not the monopoly, of power enjoyed in the temporal and spiritual spheres by the pope.' Every human creature, he asserted, is and ought to be subject to the Roman pontiff. This too may be a logical expression of the commission of Christ to Peter—but it is hardly in the humble tone of the gospel.

3 Militarily speaking, these were perhaps little more than periodical skirmishes for a century or more, between about 1120 and 1240. They are called the wars of investiture, because the issue, technically, was who has the right to invest a newly appointed bishop with the insignia of his office. The matter was of course crucial, because bishops were not only ecclesiastical pastors, they were also great feudal magnates. So kings

claimed the right to invest them with their feudal temporalities by handing them also the emblems of their spiritual authority, the ring and the crozier. This, the popes and their party disputed.

4 This was the technical canonical term: the pope made provision for filling a vacancy, he 'provided' a man to the vacancy. In the thirteenth century and again in the fourteenth, the kings of England Edward I and Edward III legislated to curb this exercise of papal authority with the Statutes of Provisors.

5 Shortly after the death of Boniface VIII a Frenchman was elected pope as Clement V (actually, as archbishop of Bordeaux he was a subject of the Duke of Aquitaine, who was Edward I, the king of England), and for a number of reasons he never reached Rome, but settled in the papal property of Avignon in the Rhône valley; and there he and his successors (all Frenchmen) stayed, to be precise, for 68 years. The period came to be known as 'the Babylonish captivity in Avignon'.

6 The Latin word is *assumuntur*; meaning, I suppose, taken up or elevated into the ranks of the bishops.

7 One might instance, in the not so very distant past, the alignment of the Church in Spain, before the Civil War, with the ruling and propertied classes. I am told that when the South African bishops were contemplating a criticism of apartheid about 1950, soon after the Nationalist party came to power, the apostolic delegate tried to dissuade them, saying it was not the policy of the Holy See openly to criticise the domestic policies and practices of governments. Most recently, in central America, and specifically in Nicaragua, the Holy See appears to have aligned itself with the more conservative elements in the local Churches, with the American administration of Ronald Reagan, and with the monied opponents of liberation theology.

6

MAGISTERIUM

The word *magisterium*, like all words, I suppose, is in itself innocuous enough. It simply means the office or role of a *magister*, a master, in all the many senses in which the word 'master' can be taken. In our context it is the meaning of 'master' as 'teacher' or 'schoolmaster' that is exclusively our concern. So for us *magisterium* means the office or role of a teacher.

Now as a technical, theological term, frequently used in official ecclesiastical documents, *magisterium* is a novelty. To the best of my knowledge it is not to be found before the nineteenth century, and it really only comes into its own with Pius XII's encyclical *Humani Generis* of 1950, as we shall see below. We are not obliged to reject it, of course, just because it is a theological novelty; most venerable theological concepts were novelties at one stage. But because it is a novelty we are obliged to greet it with some reserve, and to submit both the term and the way it is used to critical scrutiny. I do not think this has ever been done in any of the official documents which employ it. It has been done by Yves Congar, OP.[1] I propose to do it here. And to give ourselves a yardstick by which to measure its current frequent official use, I will begin by quoting from a sermon of St Augustine's, in which I came across it.

A. 'Magisterium' in Sermon 23 of St Augustine

The sermon was preached in Carthage on the anniversary of the ordination of the bishop of that city, Augustine's friend Aurelius. Many other bishops were no doubt present. The sermon begins as follows:

> Let us take it that what we have been singing to the Lord has been proposed to us as a subject to talk about. Let my sermon to you be on this point. And may the one to whom we have said *You have held my right hand, and led me along*

according to your will, and taken me up with glory (Ps 73:23), may he take our minds up to a clearer understanding, and assist us with his mercy and grace: me as I talk, you as you judge. For although to all appearances I am standing in a higher place than you, this is merely for the convenience of carrying my voice better, and in fact it is you who are in the higher place to pass judgement, and I who am being judged. We bishops are called teachers, but in many matters we seek a teacher ourselves, and we certainly don't want to be regarded as masters *(magistri)*. That is dangerous, and forbidden by the Lord himself, who says *Do not wish to be called masters, you have one master, the Christ* (Mt 23:10). So the office of master *(magisterium)* is dangerous, the state of disciple safe. That's why the psalm says *To my hearing you will give joy and exultation* (Ps 51:8). Hearing the word is safer than uttering it. That's why that man feels quite safe as *he stands and hears him, and rejoices with joy at the bridegroom's voice* (Jn 3:29).

The apostle had taken on the part of teacher because his stewardship obliged him to, and just see what he says about it: *With fear and much trembling was I among you* (1 Cor 2:3). So it is much safer that both we who speak and you who listen should realise that we are fellow-disciples under one master. Yes, it's unquestionably safer, and it helps enormously if you listen to us not as your masters but as your fellow pupils. Just see how anxiety is drummed into us by this text: *Brothers, let not most of you become masters, for all of us slip up in many ways.* Who wouldn't shudder at the apostle saying 'all of us'? And he goes on, *Whoever does not slip up in speech, this is a perfect man* (Jas 3:1–2). And who would ever dare to call himself perfect?

Well, at any rate, the one who stands and hears does not slip up in speech. As for the one who is speaking, even if he does not slip up, which is difficult enough, imagine what he suffers from his dread of slipping up! So what *you* have to do is not only listen to us speaking, but also feel for us dreading; in this way, for whatever we may say that is true (since everything true is from Truth) you will praise not us but him; and wherever, being human, we slip up, you will pray to the same 'him' for us.

He mentions *magisterium* only once, in the first paragraph, and then it is in effect to repudiate the role for himself and his fellow bishops. But the whole passage is about the problem that this raises, on which he makes a number of very pertinent observations.

In the first place, he knows that because we have only one master, Christ, all Christians, bishops and people together, are fellow disciples under that one master, and therefore they can and must and do help each other to learn. Secondly, while he cannot deny that as a bishop he has the obligation to teach, to be a teacher (the same holds good of the theologian or the catechist), he knows that the very teaching process is a kind of dialogue between teacher and pupil, in which the pupil is not merely passive but is required all the time to exercise a critical judgement. So thirdly, he tells the faithful that they are in a very real sense the *judges* of what they hear the bishops and other preachers and teachers teaching them, whether from the pulpit or in books and written documents. Fourthly, he is acutely conscious that precisely as an official teacher (he still will not allow himself to be a master) he is liable 'to slip up in speech'—or of course in the written word—and so again he asks for the help of the faithful both in praying for him and in listening to him with a sympathy that is also critical. He had no *simpliste* concept of infallibility to hide behind and give him a spurious assurance and resistance to criticism.

B. The incidence of *magisterium* in official documents

I have collected the following information by scratching about, not very scientifically, perhaps, but with some considerable pains, in the pages of Denzinger's *Enchiridion*, 33rd edition, 1965. I have found no use of the word *magisterium* before 1835, though the Roman Church is said by Innocent III in 1199 to be preeminent over other Churches *quasi magistra et mater* (Dz 774), and in the Tridentine profession of faith promulgated by Pius IV in 1564 to be *omnium ecclesiarum matrem et magistram* (Dz 1868). These are at least remote antecedents for the use of the term *magisterium*. Here then are the occasions on which the word is used up to and including its use in the encyclical *Humani Generis* in 1950.[2]

(1) 1835, in Gregory XVI's brief *Dum acerbissimas* condemning the errors of George Hermes, the *Ecclesiae magisterium* is coupled with sacred scripture, tradition, and revelation as some of the things his errors were about (Dz 2739).

(2) 1863, in Pius IX's letter *Tuas libenter* to the archbishop of Munich criticising a theological conference organised by Dr Döllinger, we have the phrases *oboedientia debita erga magisterium Ecclesiae* (Dz 2875), and *ordinario totius Ecclesiae per orbem dispersae magisterio* (2879); this means, in the context, the Church's ordinary teaching of things as divinely revealed, even though they have not been explicitly defined.

(3) 1870, in Vatican I's definition of papal infallibility, the chapter is headed *De Romani Pontificis infallibili magisterio*, and it is stated that *supremam magisterii potestatem* is contained in his apostolic primacy (Dz 3065).

(4) 1878, Leo XIII had an extra clause inserted into the profession of faith prescribed for Orientals by Benedict XIV in 1743; it accepted Vatican I's definition *de R o m a n i P o n t i f i c i s i n f a l l i b i l i m a g i s t e r i o* (Dz 2539). The spaced lettering follows Denzinger, which I presume follows the typography of the original in the *Acta Apostolicae Sedis*, or at least its emphases.

(5) 1896, in Leo XIII's encyclical *Satis Cognitum*, we have this statement: *instituit Jesus Christus in Ecclesia v i v u m, a u t h e n t i- c u m, idemque p e r e n n e m a g i s t e r i u m* (Dz 3305). We now see, as a consequence presumably of the definition of Vatican I, that the apotheosis of *magisterium* is already under way; it is given special typographical emphasis.

(6) 1907, in Pius X's encyclical *Pascendi* on modernism, it is stated that secondary statements, *si demum a supremo Ecclesiae magisterio sancitae fuerint*, constitute dogma (Dz 3482). The same idea is repeated with the variant expression *cum a magisterio publico sancitae fuerint* (Dz 3488).

(7) 1914, in Benedict XV's encyclical *Ad beatissimi Apostolorum*, on the limits of free theological discussion, it is declared: 'All know to whom the *magisterium Ecclesiae* has been given by God; to this one therefore belongs the complete right to speak as he thinks fit, when he will; the duty of the rest is religiously to comply with the speaker and to be hearers of what is said' (Dz 3625). Typographically in these last two instances *magisterium* has declined from its 1896 apogee, but substantively this last text is the most magisterial we have yet come across.

(8) 1950, in Pius XII's encyclical *Humani Generis* the term occurs at least eleven times and acquires a capital letter: Dz 3884, twice, once as *hoc sacrum Magisterium*; Dz 3885, twice, *supremam sui Magisterii potestatem* and *Magisterio ordinario*; Dz 3886, three times, *ea quae a vivo Magisterio docentur, Deus Ecclesiae suae Magis-*

terium vivum dedit, and *soli Ecclesiae Magisterio*; Dz 3887, once, *sacri Magisterii doctrina*; Dz 3892, once, *ipsum Magisterium Ecclesiae*; Dz 3896, once, *Ecclesiae Magisterium*; Dz 3897, once, *acta Magisterii Ecclesiae*.

There I ended my researches into Denzinger. '*Magisterium*' has now clearly achieved full apotheosis within the shrine of Roman theology, always with a capital M, and frequently qualified as 'sacred' or 'living'. From now on it will be paraded for our veneration with uninhibited frequency. I just note that in the *Instruction on Certain Aspects of the 'Theology of Liberation'* put out by the Congregation for the Doctrine of the Faith in 1984 it occurs five times (always with a capital M, usually in the phrase 'the Magisterium of the Church', once as 'the Roman Magisterium'), while in the *Instruction on Christian Freedom and Liberation* of the same Congregation in 1986 it also occurs five times. In an earlier and very significant Vatican document, the Apostolic Constitution *Sapientia Christiana* promulgated in 1979, I found it also five times (always with the capital M), once qualified as 'living', and once as 'authentic'. I will have some comments on these particular documents in the next section.

C. Conclusion

It is, perhaps, idle to speculate on why the term *magisterium* was so late in entering the theological scene. The mediaeval papalists were quite as committed as the nineteenth-century ultramontanes to exalting papal authority on all fronts. What restrained them from pressing into service such a useful weapon as *magisterium*? We have seen that Augustine repudiated any *magisterium* for himself and his fellow bishops. Can it be that this scruple, induced by our Lord's words in Mt 23:10, still had a restraining effect on mediaeval papalist theologians?

In any case, by the nineteenth century that scruple, if scruple it had been, was finally laid to rest. Augustine approached his duty as a teacher of Christian doctrine with fear and trembling, with an explicit sense of the possibility of his 'slipping up in speech', and above all a sense of his being a fellow pupil with the rest of the faithful at the feet of the one master, Christ. No such modest hesitations mark the employment of the term *magisterium*, let alone *Magisterium*, in the Roman documents from Gregory XVI's Brief in 1835 onwards.

The history of the word which we have just traced shows

clearly that it is a tool in the kit of the ultramontane or Roman
school of theology. The cardinal doctrine of this school has from
the beginning been the papal primacy and infallibility—to be
more precise, the pope's infallible *magisterium*. So we see the word
introduced into the official terminology in the decades leading up
to 1870, preparing the ground for the definition of the doctrine.
But the doctrine as defined at Vatican I did not quite come up to
the hopes of the ultramontanes—the opposition to it had been
rather strong and had induced the promoters of the definition to
modify it in several respects. So after the Council the word
continued to be of service to the ultramontane school in pushing
what its opponents justly call 'creeping infallibility'. That rather
staggering statement in Benedict xv's encyclical quoted above (7)
is a case in point, as well as the frequent employment of the term
in the encyclical *Humani generis* (8).

One should note that *magisterium* is never precisely defined.
This makes it easy to fuse the *magisterium* of the Church with the
magisterium of the Roman Pontiff, or of the Holy See, or the
Roman *magisterium*. This encourages the ultramontane or MP
inclination to treat all papal pronouncements as oracular, hence as
endowed with the note of infallibility. Hence once again 'creeping
infallibility'.

Perhaps the most important quality of the concept of *magisterium* as used in these documents is its essential unreality. In so far as
it means 'teaching office' (which it does), it manifestly is not and
cannot be the exclusive responsibility and right of the bishops and
the pope. To name only one activity reserved by MPs, and by
these documents, to 'the living *Magisterium* of the Church', viz.
'the authentic interpretation of Scripture': it is likely, indeed
practically certain, that few popes and not many bishops are
professional scripture scholars or biblical theologians. So
whenever popes desire an authentic interpretation of some
scriptural passage (which, to be fair, they very rarely do) they
properly consult the experts. The same is presumably true for
documents of the papal *magisterium* in other areas, the social
teaching of the popes, for example. So while of course the popes
endorse the documents, the teaching they contain which receives
the *cachet* of being the teaching of 'the Magisterium' is in fact that
of the Roman theologians. Thus it is a particular school of theology, the school of the ultramontane magisterial papalists, that is
given the privileged position of being the magisterial measure to
which all other theologians are supposed to conform.[3]

The net result is to quell, if not quench, theological debate, and to substitute for it the quasi-authoritative condemnation of the positions of one set of theologians by another set of theologians, who are by no means necessarily endowed with greater theological acumen—or greater fidelity to the whole Catholic tradition. The clearest instance of this in the recent past has been the Roman response to Latin American liberation theology. It had been evident for some years that the MP party in Rome, as indeed in Latin America also, had been very unhappy about liberation theology. So in due course the Congregation for the Doctrine of the Faith produces the *Instruction on Certain Aspects of the 'Theology of Liberation'*, clearly designed to discredit liberation theology as not being in accord with the *Magisterium*. But this document, the work of the congregation's theologians in Rome, was on several counts a very second-rate and shoddy piece of work by any respectable theological standards.[4] When it was published it was widely criticised on all sides (which indicates perhaps that the word *magisterium* is losing some of its magic). The Brazilian bishops, one has reason to believe, led a discreet but effective counter-attack, and the *Instruction* may be said already to have lapsed into oblivion. Its successor, the *Instruction on Christian Freedom and Liberation*, in practice leaves the liberation theologians free to get on with what they were doing. But it does signify that the MP party in Rome is as determined as ever to assert its control over all theological activity in the Church.

This determination to control everything from the centre, in virtue of the papal authority, is expressed even more un-equivocally—and more effectively—in that other document we noted, the Apostolic Constitution *Sapientia Christiana* promulgated in 1979 by the Congregation for Christian Education. This congregation does not receive the limelight, or hit the headlines, as much as the Congregation for the Doctrine of the Faith, but it is quite as powerful an agent of MP policy, as we are beginning to see over the case of Charles Curran. The constitution purports to be an updating of Pius XI's *Deus scientiarum Dominus* in the light of Vatican II. That document regulated the functioning of pontifical universities. This document, *Sapientia Christiana*, does the same, only more so. It is true that in the introduction it acknowledges the great diversity of cultures in the world, and remarks that the gospel must not be tied to any one particular culture, and admits that this diversity seems to call for pluralism rather than uniformity in theological education, so that

it is very difficult to draft common legislation for Catholic insti-
tutes of higher learning, especially faculties of theology, throughout the world. Nonetheless, in the interests of 'a substantial unity'
(by which it means a centrally controlled uniformity) it proceeds
to do just that. In art. 6 it lays down that 'only Universities and
Faculties canonically erected or approved by the Holy See, and
governed according to the rule of this Constitution, have the right
of conferring academic degrees which have canonical validity,
saving the special rights of the Pontifical Biblical Commission'.
Art. 12 declares that the Chancellor of such an institute, usually
the local bishop, represents the Holy See to the institute and the
institute to the Holy See—i.e. the bishop of the local Church does
not preside over the Catholic university attached to his Church in
his own right, but only as an agent of the Holy See. Art. 18 lays
down that the Rector or President of such an institute is nomin-
ated or at least confirmed by the Congregation for Christian
Education. Of the teaching staff, after several articles listing the
required qualifications, and reminding them that they must carry
out their duties 'in full communion with the authentic Magisterium of the Church, above all of the Roman Pontiff' (art. 26:2),
art. 27:2 rules that they may only be granted tenure or promoted
to 'the supreme didactic order' if they have received a *nihil obstat*
from the Holy See. Thus the strictest possible control from the
centre, from the school of Roman theology, over the teaching of
all Catholic theology is satisfactorily ensured. Not much room
here for pluralism or cultural diversity.

Conclusion

We have seen St Augustine repudiating any *magisterium* for
himself as a bishop, while accepting his responsibility as a bishop
to teach. So presumably he felt that the word meant something
more than just teaching office or role. In its modern usage I think
we can see what that something more is; it is the suggestion of
infallibly authoritative teaching. That was what Augustine wisely
repudiated, because Mt 23:10 suggests plainly that such teaching
is the peculiar prerogative of Christ alone. The rest of us, popes
and all, are all fellow disciples, fellow pupils at the feet of the one
Master. Human teaching, which is of course inseparable from
human learning, is far too complex a business ever to be able to
claim infallible authority, or authoritative infallibility.

So in advocating the removal of the term *magisterium* from the
ecclesiastical vocabulary, am I also advocating a repudiation of

any claim to ecclesiastical and papal infallibility? No. What I am maintaining is that infallibility is something that may qualify an act of *judgement*, not an act of teaching. I find infallibility therefore in certain ecclesiastical judgements. For example I claim that I, together with all the faithful, in virtue of our participating in the prophetic gift of Jesus Christ (*Lumen Gentium*, 12), am making an infallibly true judgement when I assert the truth of the Apostles' creed, or the Nicene creed. I claim that bishops in Council, in virtue of their sharing in Christ's prophetic authority, have made infallibly true judgements whenever they have formally defined any doctrine as part of the Christian faith. I claim likewise that the pope, in virtue of his special sharing in Christ's prophetic authority, makes an infallibly true judgement when, for example, he defines the doctrine of the Immaculate Conception or of the Assumption into heaven of the Virgin Mary as part of the Christian faith. But infallibility in the hurly-burly business of teaching, even teaching by a pope, let alone by papal theologians—there my natural human scepticism intervenes. In this direction the pretensions of the magisterial papalist school of theologians rapidly lose credibility.

Moreover it has commonly been taught—and it is very sound teaching, and I challenge MPs to repudiate it—that it is precisely the formal definitions of Councils, and of popes speaking *ex cathedra*, that are binding on the faith of Catholics, that are infallible in other words, and not the reasons and arguments adduced in support. This bears out my preference for the word 'judgement' over *magisterium* as specifying the area in which infallibility operates. When delivering their judgements, judges very properly give their reasons, and in doing so they often expound important legal doctrine—in other words they teach. But their legal doctrine, while listened to with due respect by the legal profession, will not be considered as binding, as constituting a precedent that has to be followed, in the same way as their actual judgements are. So too we must distinguish between the teaching of popes, bishops and councils (which is in fact, materially speaking, usually the teaching of their theologians), and their definitive judgements for which they alone are personally responsible. The latter we must accept in obedience as binding, and in some cases as infallible. The former, while we listen to it with due respect, we should also listen to, as Augustine tells us, as its judges, that is to say with a critical attention, and should never regard as simply putting an end to theological or ecclesiastical debate.

NOTES

1 Yves Congar, OP, 'Pour une histoire sémantique du terme "magisterium"', *Revue des sciences philosophiques et théologiques*, vol. 60 (1976), pp. 85–98. Unlike me, he is not concerned in his article to make any judgements on the modern use of the word.

2 I here give the English of the phrases quoted in Latin, except for the titles of the documents quoted. I do not translate *magisterium*.

B *quasi magistra et mater*—as mistress (= authoritative teacher) and mother;

  omnium ecclesiarum matrem et magistram—mother and mistress of all the churches.

B (1) *Ecclesiae magisterium*—the *magisterium* of the Church.

(2) *oboedientia debita erga magisterium Ecclesiae*—the obedience due to the *magisterium* of the Church;

  ordinario totius Ecclesiae per orbem dispersae magisterio—to the ordinary *magisterium* of the Church dispersed throughout the world.

(3) *De Romani Pontificis infallibili magisterio*—on the Roman Pontiff's infallible *magisterium*;

  supremam magisterii potestatem—the supreme authority of the *magisterium*.

(4) as above in (3).

(5) *instituit Jesus Christus . . . m a g i s t e r i u m*—Jesus Christ established in the Church a l i v i n g, a u t h e n t i c, and likewise p e r p e t u a l m a g i s t e r i u m.

(6) *si demum a supremo Ecclesiae magisterio sancitae fuerint*—if they are finally sanctioned by the supreme *magisterium* of the Church;

  cum a magisterio publico sancitae fuerint—when they have been sanctioned by the public *magisterium*.

(7) *magisterium Ecclesiae*—the *magisterium* of the Church. See below, note 3.

(8) *hoc sacrum Magisterium*—this sacred *Magisterium*;

  supremam sui Magisterii potestatem—the supreme authority of their *Magisterium*;

  Magisterio ordinario—by the ordinary *Magisterium*. Here, incidentally, there is a notable and dubious extension of the meaning of 'ordinary *magisterium*' from what it had in Pius IX's letter in (2) above. There it meant the common teaching by the Church of doctrines commonly assumed to be of faith—e.g. the resurrection of the dead. Here it means *any* papal teaching in encyclicals that does not qualify, according to the very strict conditions of *Pastor Aeternus*, as infallible. What it appears to be saying is: 'It may not be formally infallible; but you must treat it as if it were'. That is pure creeping infallibility.

  ea quae a vivo Magisterio docentur—things that are taught by the living *Magisterium*;

Deus Ecclesiae suae Magisterium vivum dedit—God gave his Church a living *Magisterium*;

    soli Ecclesiae Magisterio—only to the Church's *Magisterium*;
    sacri Magisterii doctrina—the doctrine of the sacred *Magisterium*;
    ipsum Magisterium Ecclesiae—the *Magisterium* itself of Church;
    Ecclesiae Magisterium—the Church's *Magisterium*;
    acta Magisterii Ecclesiae—the acts of the Church's *Magisterium*.

3. For example, with reference to the quotation in B (7) above from Benedict xv's encyclical *Ad beatissimi Apostolorum*, I really cannot believe that this stark statement of the most extreme, authoritarian, if not arrogant, magisterial papalism, this view of teaching as a crudely simple process of the master speaking and the pupil meekly saying 'Ja, baas' (the Southern African context in which I am writing inevitably casts a harsher light on the whole authoritarian ethos of magisterial papalism)—I really cannot believe that this statement expresses the personal sentiments of that pope himself. It is more likely the work of advisers and/or theologians in the Secretariat of State, or other Vatican department, whom he inherited from his predecessor, Pius x, only a few months deceased. My guess would be that it represents their attempt to ensure that the policies of the new pontificate did not depart too rapidly, and from their point of view catastrophically, from those of the old.

4 Such a severe criticism of an official Church document requires some substantiation. When the *Instruction*, was published in September 1984, it received wide comment in Catholic journals, and it was also circulated (this should be said to the Congregation of the Doctrine of the Faith's credit) to bishops' conferences for their comments. Bishops' conferences, very naturally and properly, consulted their local theologians, of whom I in Southern Africa was one.

Let me begin with a comment in *The Tablet*, 8 September 1984, and then go on to some of the comments we in Southern Africa offered to our bishops' conferences. *The Tablet*'s first substantial criticism is: 'It is noteworthy that the Vatican instruction fails to include any word of regret and repentance for the past record of the Church in Latin America'. The whole magisterial attitude and style, of course, make expressions of regret and repentance almost impossible. Then after questioning a number of the assertions in the *Instruction*, *The Tablet* goes on to put it in a context which casts doubt on its claim to be received precisely as doctrinal instruction; it suggests that it was issued (together with its successor) 'as part of a concerted strategy to bring the Latin Americans into line', in other words, as an instrument of papal *policy*. But can we possibly accept that papal *policy*—which changes according to circumstances, and from one pope to the next—is to be accorded the same kind of unquestioning submission as is claimed for papal teaching? And is not the assumption that you can cast the mantle of papal teaching over papal policies precisely the kind of fatal error that a system like ultramontane magisterial papalism is bound to end in?

One of my colleagues submitted to his bishops' conference a little analysis of the *Instruction*'s employment of inverted commas. They are frequently used in a straightforward way to indicate quotations, or a term as distinct from the thing signified by the term, as here for instance: 'The expression "Theology of Liberation" refers etc.' (*Instruction*, III, 3). But they are also employed in that much less straightforward way beloved of newspaper columnists and other propagandists to suggest scepticism about the object thus enclosed. The equivalent technique in speeches and broadcasting is to stigmatise something or someone as 'so-called'. Thus the very title: *Instruction on certain aspects of the 'Theology of Liberation'*. It isn't a *real* theology, you see; or it isn't a theology of *genuine* liberation. And indeed every time theology of liberation, theologies of liberation, or theologians of liberation are mentioned in the document, they are put in these tokens of superior scepticism. Such use of one of the cheaper techniques of popular knock-about debate by a document claiming magisterial authority is, I maintain, rightly to be denounced as shoddy.

The criticisms which I submitted to my bishops' conference were more varied and more severe, ranging from noting the frequent careless-ness and occasional error in the English translation (for which the Con-gregation cannot refuse responsibility) to more substantial flaws. Of these I will just mention three:

(1) On IV, 12, which runs, 'New Testament revelation teaches us that sin is the greatest evil, since it strikes man in the heart of his personality. The first liberation, to which all others must make reference, is that from sin'—I commented:

> This short section is so general that it is almost entirely lacking in content. It is like saying 'Good is to be done, and evil to be avoided'. It is true, but does it get us any further? And in any case, is its language theologically sound? *Peccatum esse summum malum* (sin is the greatest evil). But St Thomas Aquinas (where does he fit in the '*Magisterium*'?) argues very forcefully in *S. Th.* 1a, 49, 3 that we cannot say there is any *summum malum* corresponding to the *summum bonum* which is God. Once you start talking like that, you are on the way to Manichaean dualism. It is noteworthy that the section says 'New Testament revelation teaches' without giving any actual reference—wisely, no doubt. And then, '*sin* is the greatest evil'; but what kind of sin? Which sin? Committed by whom? Original sin? Again we are half in the world of platonic forms, with some kind of reality called 'Sin-in-general'— committed no doubt by 'Man-in-general'. The document does seem to have fallen into the trap of assuming that 'sin' is a univocal concept. The *primum analogatum*, surely, is *aversio a Deo*, sinning against the love of God. And its immediate consequence is aliena-tion, from God and from fellow creatures. This, if not exactly a

Marxist concept, is one that might permit of a certain dialogue with Marxists.

(2) This brings me to my second criticism. From VII onwards the *Instruction* rebukes Christians whom 'Impatience and a desire for results has led . . . to turn to what they call "marxist analysis" '. It then goes on to argue that it is quite impossible to take one bite out of the Marxist cherry without swallowing the whole. It says so in so many words: 'Thus no separation ;f the parts of this epistemologically unique complex is possible'. Now this is certainly the most extraordinary piece of magisterial doctrine I have ever come across. Marxism must indeed be epistemologically unique if this is the case. Tertullian, I suppose, in his fiercer and more Montanist moments, would have said the same about all pagan philosophy: 'What has Athens to do with Jerusalem?' But most of the Fathers borrowed extensively and happily from Stoicism and Platonism without thereby feeling logically obliged to swallow those systems whole; the scholastics did the same with the philosophy of Aristotle. Why is it suddenly impossible with Marx? One can only suspect it is because some of the Congregation for the Doctrine of the Faith's theologians (I resist the temptation to clothe them with inverted commas) are borrowing from the philosophy of anti-communism, which is the stock-in-trade of journals of the extreme right, and of political crusaders like Jerry Falwell. Let us, to clinch the matter and my criticism, analyse the *Instruction*'s logic on this point. The reason given for the sentence I quoted earlier in this paragraph is this: 'The ideological principles come prior to the study of the social reality and are presupposed in it. Thus no separation of the parts of this epistemologically unique complex is possible'. Why not? Because 'If p, then q; but q, therefore p'. But never mind the logic. The point is that now we can dismiss 'liberation theology' as Marxist, and therefore atheist and totalitarian and materialist *simpliciter*.

(3) The *Instruction* has some very odd things to say about history in IX, 3: 'According to this conception, the class struggle is the driving force of history. History thus becomes a central notion. It will be affirmed that God himself makes history. It will be added that there is only one history, one in which the distinction between the history of salvation and profane history is no longer necessary. To maintain the distinction would be to fall into "dualism". Affirmations such as these reflect historicist immanentism. Thus there is a tendency to identify the kingdom of God and its growth with the human liberation movement, and to make history itself the subject of its own development, as a progress of the self-redemption of man by means of the class struggle. This identification is in opposition to the faith of the Church as it has been reaffirmed by the Second Vatican Council'. On this I commented:

A paragraph of stupendous confusion. 'History thus becomes a central notion.' For a historical religion like ours I thought it always has been and certainly should be. But the ultramontane

Roman theology which is presumably most powerfully represented in the CDF has always shown a combination of ignorance,
fear and contempt for history. It is suggested that 'the distinction
between the history of salvation and profane history' is doctrinally
obligatory. In my view, unless it is regarded as a purely *material*
distinction, made for convenience like the division of a book into
chapters, it is doctrinally and theologically monstrous, as it inevitably tends to exclude divine providence from what it calls 'profane
history'. The Vatican Council text referred to, *Lumen Gentium*
9–17, is the chapter on the People of God. This certainly does not
require us to make a formal distinction between sacred and profane
history. A purely secular, this-worldly philosophy of history is
obviously in opposition to the faith of the Church—and possibly
this is what our text means by 'historicist immanentism'. But
which liberation theologians adopt it?

I said I would only mention three of the points I made in my critique,
submitted to the bishops, and I will keep my word. In conclusion I will
only add one extrinsic criticism of that particular document. It was
received in South Africa with dismay by all black Catholics who came to
know about it, by all black Christians who knew about it; and it was
received by the South African government and its supporters with im-
mense satisfaction. Similar responses were no doubt elicited from corresponding groups in North and Latin America.

7

PASTOR AETERNUS, 1870:
A CRITICAL EXAMINATION

At the end of Chapter 5 I said that I would in due course proceed to a critical comparison between the Constitutions *Pastor Aeternus* of the first Vatican Council and *Lumen Gentium* of the second. Having now come to that point, I think it is in fact more convenient to devote a chapter each to the examination of these documents. So here we shall be confining ourselves to the document of 1870.

But it will be useful to begin by observing a common, and at the same time contrasting, pattern or setting for the two Vatican Councils that in turn produced these documents. In both there was a minority of opponents to the dominant party, too large to be ignored, whose criticisms had to be met. The result in both texts is a certain incoherence, occasional twists and turns, changes of emphasis and so on. The difference between the two Councils is that at Vatican I the dominant party was the ultramontane curial party, while at Vatican II, to almost everyone's surprise, this party had dwindled to being the minority of opponents. But having the curial members of the Council as their core, they were in a much stronger position than the minority in 1870, and remained almost as effectively in control of Church government after the second Council as after the first. No, I am happy to have to say that that is an exaggeration; but let it stand for the moment.

My aim quite frankly will be to *emphasise* the modifications of the 1870 definitions which the critics managed to get incorporated into the text—and then to show how the MPs in power have consistently ignored them and succeeded in practically erasing them from the popular mind; while on the other hand in the next chapter I will persistently *downplay* the modifications of the text of *Lumen Gentium* that the MPs, now a minority, managed to have inserted. If this seems partisan, well of course it is. It is only countering the similar and opposite process that the MPs have been practising all along. In addition there is this particular point: *Pastor Aeternus* is a text of dogmatic definitions, and definitions which are binding on our faith call for the most precise and strict interpretation, in order not to lay on people's shoulders burdens that are too heavy to bear (something Newman accused the ultramontanes of his day of being quite indifferent to). *Lumen Gentium*, on the other hand, is a doctrinal Constitution without any formal definitions in it. With such a document what has to be ascertained is the general drift or direction of its teaching: and this is simply obscured, not to say thwarted, by most of the MP modifications the text contains, though it is they that receive all the emphasis in post-conciliar MP references to the document.

A. The context of *Pastor Aeternus*

In what follows I am indebted to an article by Dom Lambert Beauduin, OSB, *L'unité de l'Eglise et le Concile du Vatican*, which he contributed to the book *L'Eglise et Unité* (Lille, 1948), and which was reprinted in a publication of the Vatican Library to mark the centenary of Vatican I in 1969, *De Doctrina Concilii Vaticani Primi*. It is in that volume that I have read it. Dom Lambert was one of the leading Catholic ecumenists before Vatican II, and his concerns are basically the same as mine—to counteract the ultramontane oversimplifications of the 1870 definitions which dominated Catholic textbooks and catechisms at the time—and Catholic thought and language generally—and which were ecumenically untenable.

Vatican I had been prepared for by a theological commission set up by Pius IX several years beforehand, a commission recruited, says Dom Lambert, from all the theology faculties of the whole world and all the religious orders. So it was not a purely Roman commission, as were the preparatory commissions of Vatican II. The Council was intended to produce a dogmatic Constitution on the Church, and the commission prepared a draft schema for this, *De Ecclesia Christi*, in fifteen chapters. Of these, only chapter 11 dealt with the primacy of the Roman Pontiff, and this did not mention papal infallibility. Evidently the commission did not think a definition on this point would be opportune, presumably because they did not find a sufficient consensus in the Church on the point.

But the Council, so carefully prepared, had not been sitting for many months before it became clear that it would not be able to sit much longer. The Franco-Prussian War was looming on the horizon; it was only the presence of a French garrison that preserved the independence of Rome and its environs as the remnant of the old Papal States; and as soon as they were withdrawn every one knew that Rome would be occupied by the forces of the new Italian state.

There would therefore be no possibility of debating the whole of the schema *De Ecclesia Christi*. So the ultramontane party being in the ascendant, actively assisted by Pius IX himself, the decision was made to proceed on chapter 11 alone, and to add a section on papal infallibility. Thus the Roman primacy and papal infallibility were discussed without being given their proper ecclesiological context. Dom Lambert is concerned to point out to the separated brethren that all this is a kind of historical accident, and that in fact Catholic doctrine about the papacy must be seen in a wider ecclesiological context. He is quite right; but I am making also the rather more polemical point that this historical accident suited the ultramontane MPs very well, because in their view Catholic doctrine about the papacy to all intents and purposes *is* ecclesiology—which could almost be renamed papology.

For of course, given that historical situation, quite another decision could have been reached; simply to adjourn the Council, and postpone the discussion of the schema *De Ecclesia Christi* altogether to another day, because it was really inappropriate to define doctrine about papal primacy and infallibility without giving it its proper context. And this was more or less the line taken at the Council by the considerable party who came to be known as the Inopportunists.

Which brings us to the immediate context of *Pastor Aeternus*, the line-up of the parties in the Council which debated it. Beauduin sketches three 'tendencies': the extreme ultramontanes, who wanted a sweeping definition of infallibility (their 'whip', in Parliamentary language, was Archbishop Manning of Westminster[1]); the moderate infallibilists; and the more or less radical opponents of the definition, above all of infallibility. I would draw the lines a little differently: the ultramontanes, some extreme like Manning, some moderate, who wanted the doctrine defined; the inopportunists, who believed in the doctrines, but did not think they were ripe for definition (Newman supported this party, and several English bishops at the Council, notably Ullathorne, and the French bishop of Orleans, Dupanloup); and those of the old Gallican school, of whom there were perhaps more among the Austrians and Hungarians than the French. Most of these left Rome a few days before the final votes in order not to make the lack of consensus too glaring. The one whose claim to immortal fame is that he stayed to vote *non placet* was the Bishop of Little Rock, Arkansas.

B. The text of *Pastor Aeternus*[2]

It is worth a passing observation that the Constitution is still entitled 'De Ecclesia Christi', although it is in fact no longer so. Whether this was just an oversight, or a kind of declaration of an intention that had been frustrated, I do not know. But at any rate it was assuredly not done in order to enable us to identify 'Church' with 'Roman pontiff'.

The Constitution has four chapters, and defines in turn four doctrines of faith: that Christ instituted Peter prince of the apostles and visible head of the whole Church militant; that Peter's primacy is continued in the Roman pontiffs as his successors; the nature of the Roman primacy; the Roman pontiff's infallible *magisterium*. I will make no comments on the first two chapters, but will begin with a few observations on the Constitution as a whole, and its introduction.

It is worth noting, as a matter of style, which is a good indicator to the general spirit of the times, that the acts of the first Vatican Council are as it were uttered by the pope himself in the first person plural, 'with the approval of the Council'. The same style will be followed, more formally and less flamboyantly by the second Vatican Council. Now this style cannot be said to be traditional. It was not followed by Trent, where the subject of all the decrees was 'This sacred ecumenical and general Tridentine Synod, legitimately assembled in the Holy Spirit'. At Florence a hundred years before Trent, it was again the pope pronouncing with the approval of the council, and that presumably was the model for Vatican I. But Florence was a quite deliberate papalist reaction against the conciliarist Council of Basle. So Vatican I, in this meekly followed by Vatican II, is deliberately taking up a papalist, anti-conciliarist precedent. The Tridentine style certainly has the far greater weight of tradition behind it, all the ecumenical councils of the first millennium. The model for the Florentine/Vatican style will have been the regular Roman synods that had met under the pope from time immemorial, and in the twelfth century had blossomed into the general, i.e. Western,

councils of the Lateran that have come to have an ecumenical
status bestowed upon them. This status is however queried by
some theologians, and has never, of course, been recognised by
the Orthodox, for whom these are just Latin councils, no more
and no less.

The reason the Constitution gives for the institution of the
Petrine primacy is 'that the episcopate itself might be one and
undivided' (Dz 3051). I think a more mature ecclesiology would
see the unity of the Churches as the purpose of the primacy of the
Roman Church, rather than the unity of the episcopate as the
purpose of the primacy of the Roman pontiff.

1. On the import and meaning of the Roman primacy (*Pastor Aeternus*, chapter 3)

The chapter consists of five paragraphs and a canon, i.e. a dogmatic 'enactment' to which an anathema is attached. It is negative in
form: 'If any one says this, that and the other, let him be anathema'; so you construe the defined doctrine, or dogma, from the
opposite. It is the general presumption that it is only and precisely
these dogmatic canons of Councils that are binding on faith—are
infallible statements of dogmatic truth. But this is too hard and
fast an axiom to be wholly acceptable, though it can be a useful
rule of thumb. What is a very sound principle of interpretation is
that the arguments adduced in support of such dogmatic definitions are not binding like the definitions themselves.

The first paragraph (Dz 3059) simply reaffirms the definition of
the Council of Florence (Dz 1307, 6 July 1439), at which an
abortive reunion between the Latins and the Greeks was negoti-
ated. I shall quote it in full, because it really says all that needs to be
said about the primacy of the Roman pontiff, and the question
arises why in 1870 it was thought necessary to add the second
paragraph of chapter 3. The first paragraph, then, runs:

> Wherefore . . . we renew the definitions of the ecumenical
> Council of Florence, according to which it is to be believed
> by all the faithful of Christ 'that the holy Apostolic See and
> the Roman Pontiff hold the primacy over the whole world,
> and that the Roman Pontiff is the successor of blessed Peter,
> the prince of the Apostles, and the true vicar of Christ and
> head of the whole Church and father and teacher of all
> Christians; and that to him in blessed Peter full authority for

feeding, ruling and governing the universal Church was
entrusted by our Lord Jesus Christ; as is also contained in the
acts of ecumenical councils and the sacred canons'.

It is worth observing that at Florence this was the first of two
paragraphs reaffirming the order of the ancient patriarchal sees,
giving Constantinople the second place after Rome. The vehe-
ment objection of Leo the Great to Chalcedon's doing just this in
451 had long been overruled and forgotten.

So, once again, this seems to say all that needs to be said. Leo's
doctrine of the *plenitudo potestatis* is reaffirmed; the bishop of
Rome has a divinely imposed responsibility for all the Churches
(or for the universal Church, as it is put here, with that mediaeval
declension from a just appreciation of the reality of local Churches): and with that responsibility he has the appropriate fullness
of authority—an authority to which nothing, in case of necessity,
is *ultra vires*.

But this did not satisfy the ultramontanes of 1870 (it had proved
too much for the Greeks almost as soon as they had put their
signatures to it—and not all of them did; the union was repudiated as soon as Constantinople fell to the Turks in 1453). They
added paragraph 2, to dot the *is* and cross the *ts* with canonical
precision. Florence used general words, 'feeding', 'ruling', 'governing', the pope being 'father' and 'teacher' of all Christians, to
designate the *plena potestas*. Any further canonical concepts would
be out of place, above all because the Greeks had a very different
canon law from the Latins, but in particular because the canonical
modalities of the papal *plena potestas* varied according to which
particular other Churches he was dealing with. His everyday
canonical relationship with the bishop of Orvieto, for example,
would be much more stringent, more obviously that of superior
giving orders to subordinate, than his relationships with the
archbishops of Toledo, Lyons or Canterbury; and these in turn
more directive than his canonical relationships with the patriarchs
of Constantinople, or the bishops of any Greek Churches.

But one almost gets the impression that the ultramontanes of
1870, and especially the canonists among them, wished to eliminate all tiresome distinctions of this kind, and place all bishops in
their relations with the Holy See on the same footing as our
bishop of Orvieto. And so this second paragraph defines this
universal and full authority of the pope over all Christians and all
Churches as 'ordinary' and 'immediate', and insists that 'all pas-

tors and faithful, of whatever rite and dignity, . . . are bound (a very strong word, *obstringuntur*) by the duty of hierarchical subordination and true obedience' towards it (Dz 3060).

Now in fact this strong, this domineering language (the language of law, when asserting authority, always tends to be domineering) adds nothing to the 'full authority' of Florence and the previous paragraph, for the simple reason that it is logically impossible to add to fullness. What it does in practice is to tell all other bishops, from the patriarch of Constantinople down, 'You must never argue with the pope or his curial advisers and officials; you just have to do what he tells you; you are in effect no more than his agents and representatives, the satraps of the provinces of his spiritual empire'.

A crucial word the paragraph introduces which I forgot to mention just now is 'jurisdiction'; the pope has a universal jurisdiction that is ordinary and immediate. This is the language of canon law. The influence of canon lawyers on theology (in our case ecclesiology) has always been incalculably disastrous. Congar tells us (note 1 on Chapter 6 above) that it was German canonists at the beginning of the nineteenth century who launched *magisterium* on its baleful theological career.

Another very obvious result of this strong canonical language was the raising of hackles all round. Orthodox, Anglican and Protestant hackles, first of all, hackles, it may be said, that will never be lowered as long as they think that to achieve union with Rome they would be required to subscribe to statements couched in such language. But secondly, political hackles of eminent men like Bismarck and Gladstone. To them immediately after the Council apologetic texts had to be addressed: a letter of the German bishops rebutting Bismarck's assertion that as a result of *Pastor Aeternus* (and he must have had chapter 3, paragraph 2 primarily in mind) the Roman Church had swallowed up all other local Churches, and the pope taken over as the immediate bishop of Cologne, Mainz etc., with the so-called bishops of these places being in fact no more than his vicars-general; in England Newman's *Letter to the Duke of Norfolk*, in much the same sense.

In effect these apologetic texts (the German bishops' letter received the formal approval and thanks of Pius IX himself in March 1875) are busy explaining away this paragraph 2 of chapter 3: all this language is strictly canonical, and so we must realise that in this context 'ordinary' and 'immediate' do not mean what 'ordinary' and 'immediate' ordinarily mean; no more is being asserted about the primacy than was asserted at Florence, etc., etc. And it must be acknowledged that poor benighted Protestants like Gladstone and Bismarck had some excuse for their 'mis-understandings', when one discovers that they were shared by so many devout Roman Catholics zealous for the pope. Dom Lambert tells us, sorrowfully, in the article cited at the beginning of this chapter, that 'the Bishop of Strasbourg wrote in March 1943 a pastoral letter to the people of his diocese which began with these words: "The supreme head of the Church, first bishop of the diocese of Strasbourg, Pius XII, has just solemnly consecrated . . ." '. So much for Pius IX having approved of the German bishops pointing out to Bismarck that the definition of the primacy in *Pastor Aeternus* did *not* make the pope bishop of Cologne or Mainz, or for that matter Strasbourg.

But thirdly, the hackles of many of the bishops at the Council were raised by this paragraph; and to such effect that they secured the insertion into the text of the third paragraph of this complex chapter (Dz 3061). Now the MPs are obliged definitely to back-track: 'So far', it states, 'is this authority of the Supreme Pontiff from interfering with that ordinary and immediate authority of episcopal jurisdiction by which the bishops . . . the successors of the Apostles, feed and rule the flocks entrusted to them as true pastors, that on the contrary this authority of theirs is asserted, strengthened and vindicated by the supreme and universal pastor, according to the words of St Gregory the Great: "My honour is the honour of the universal Church. My honour is the solid vigour of my brethren. Then I am truly honoured when due honour is not denied to any one of them" [*Ep.* 30: PL 77, 933C]'.

Now this is an excellent statement of principle, indeed of Catholic doctrine. But one is bound to say that it is not a statement of MP principle or practice. In fact, if it is taken as a statement of things as they are, not just of principle, it is unfortunately not true. During the last millennium the steady extension of papal authority, the ever increasing exercise of the Holy See's ordinary and immediate jurisdiction, has made vast inroads on the authority of the bishops of the Latin Churches, and of the oriental Churches in communion with Rome,[3] and continued to do so without a qualm after 1870. The language of the poor bishop of Strasbourg shows how little notice would be taken of this paragraph in the standard theological education of the clergy after 1870. As for the quotation from Gregory the Great's letter to the Patriarch of Alexandria: the whole tone and drift of that letter is so contrary to MP ultramontanism, that I give a translation of the whole letter in Appendix 1. What Pope Gregory was in fact doing was protesting against the exaggerated titles of honour with which Patriarch Eulogius had addressed him, calling him 'universal pope' and talking about what he, Gregory, had 'commanded'.

The fourth and fifth paragraphs of chapter 3 need not detain us. The fourth is directed at secular authorities and insists on the right of the Holy See to free communication with all other Churches as an implication of the primacy. The fifth declares the Roman pontiff to be supreme and final judge in all Church cases, from whom there is no appeal to any higher tribunal, and certainly not to any Council as being superior to the pope. Here an old battle is being fought once more against conciliarism and Gallicanism. On this point, though, it is worth remarking, that as the judge of final appeal, the pope should not, in the interests of natural justice, through the tribunals of the Holy See ever try cases in the first instance. I do not think the practice of many of the Roman congregations measures up very well to this requirement.

2. On the Roman Pontiff's infallible *magisterium* (*Pastor Aeternus*, chapter 4)

The reader will remember from section A of this chapter that the original draft *De Ecclesia Christi* dedicated one of its fifteen chapters (chapter 11) to the Roman primacy, without making any mention in that chapter, or indeed elsewhere, of papal infallibility. When chapter 11 was brought on for discussion by itself, owing to the threatening political situation, this extra chapter was added, at the express desire of Pius IX himself, enthusiastically supported of course by ardent ultramontanes like Archbishop Manning. It is rather longer than chapter 3, running in Denzinger to eleven paragraphs, including the final anathema, which is just two lines. Some of the paragraphs could easily be run together.

It begins by giving its authorities for the doctrine of papal infallibility, and is at pains to quote above all 'those ecumenical Councils in which the East came together with the West in a union of faith and charity' (Dz 3065). Unfortunately, the three councils it quotes in the following paragraphs (Dz 3066–3068) are councils which the East today does not recognise: Constantinople IV, 869, which deposed Photius, patriarch of that city, who is today one of the heroes of Orthodoxy; Lyons II, 1274, which achieved an ephemeral union with the Byzantine emperor Michael Palaeologus; and once again, Florence, 1439, the same text as was quoted in chapter 3.

In any case, the text quoted as coming from Constantinople IV did not emanate from that Council, but was an abbreviated quotation of the *Formula* of Pope Hormisdas, sent by him to Constantinople in 515, to terminate a much earlier breach between Rome and that city, known as the Acacian schism.

These observations are not intended to discredit the authorities quoted, but only to illustrate the characteristic ultramontane ineptitude at, or indifference to, the hard facts of history. The quotation from the *Formula* of Hormisdas might indeed have carried more weight with the Orthodox if it had been given its correct ascription, since the reconciliation it effected between East and West has never since been repudiated by the Orthodox, as have the condemnation of Photius and the brief and superficial unions of the Middle Ages.

There are some hard historical facts which were certainly being much discussed in 1870, and which must have had their effect on the eventual definition, but which are not mentioned in this chapter. They concern Popes Liberius (352–366), Vigilius (537–555), and above all Honorius I (625–638). All three subscribed to formulae of very doubtful orthodoxy, the first two under severe, and in the case of Vigilius brutal, imperial pressure.[4] There is the further interesting case of the mediaeval Pope John XXII (1316–1334), who not only vigorously repudiated any doctrine of papal infallibility in his long quarrel with the Franciscan Spirituals,[5] but also put out a doctrine about the state of the blessed before the resurrection of the dead, which just before his death he formally retracted, and which his successor Benedict XII formally condemned. These cases clearly required the laying down of very strict conditions to be met before a papal statement could be claimed to be infallible, and these conditions were duly stated in the definition. They were far more stringent than ultramontanes wanted, ultramontanes like W. G. Ward, for example, of whom it was said that he would like to receive an infallible pronouncement every morning with *The Times* at his breakfast table.[6]

After quoting its authorities, the chapter goes on in the next paragraph (Dz 3069) to give the idealised MP myth of Church history: according to this myth, the popes have always governed the universal Church exactly as they govern the Latin Church today. All the best initiatives have come from them; they have orchestrated and elicited all the teachings of all the ecumenical councils, and consulted the bishops in local councils, and always been referred to by bishops from all over the Christian world in difficult cases, and always defined the true doctrine to be held according to the orthodox apostolic tradition. It is all very remote from the hurly-burly and the painful ambiguities of real history. But it does at least make clear that popes never have defined doctrines all by themselves and on their own. The business of defining doctrine is necessarily a co-operative one, involving many other institutional organisms of the Church besides the Roman pontiff. His contribution has (sometimes) been to give the whole transaction the final touch of certainty. That is the truth enshrined in this ultramontane historical myth.

The next paragraph (Dz 3070) goes on to make a very important clarification that is not always well understood by Catholics, let alone by other Christians. It states that the assistance given the pope by the Holy Spirit in what is later called the 'charism' of infallibility does not enable him to make public newly revealed doctrines—it is not a prophetic charism, in other words, in the strict sense—but only enables him to declare without error what has been revealed, or 'faithfully to preserve and expound the deposit of faith'. In other words the pope, when he makes an infallible definition, speaks not as the mouthpiece and representative of God, but as the mouthpiece and representative of the Church.[7] It is in fact in the next paragraph (Dz 3071) that it is called a 'charism of truth and of *never-failing faith*'. When he defines, the pope speaks precisely as a *believer*, not as a revealer.

So we come now to the text of the definition itself, which we must give in full (Dz 3074). It runs as follows:

> Therefore . . . we teach and define to be a divinely revealed dogma, that the Roman Pontiff, when he speaks *ex cathedra*, that is when in the performance of his office of pastor and teacher of all Christians, by his supreme Apostolic authority he defines a doctrine about faith or morals to be held by the whole Church, through the divine assistance promised to him in blessed Peter is endowed with that infallibility with which the divine Redeemer wished his Church to be equipped in the definition of doctrine about faith and morals; and therefore that such definitions of the Roman Pontiff are irreformable of themselves, and not as a result of the consent of the Church.

Then follows the formal anathema against anyone who should presume to contradict this definition.

It is a long and complex sentence, which I have avoided simplifying in the English translation. Let us take it bit by bit, beginning with the main statement.

> The Roman Pontiff . . . is endowed with that infallibility with which the divine Redeemer wished his Church to be equipped in the definition of doctrine about faith and morals:

This is an absolutely fundamental point, which is often overlooked in arguments on the topic. Papal infallibility is part and parcel of what we could call ecclesial infallibility. Once again, the pope here is the representative of the Church, not of God, he expresses the Church's faith, not God's revelation. As we shall see when we come to Vatican II, the Church's infallibility is something all the faithful share in, just as we share in the Church's faith. It is a statement of our certainty about the faith. This certainty is not total or unlimited, not a certainty about anything and everything. There are many things to do with our religion and our beliefs that if we are wise we admit to real uncertainty about, like what the Bible means in this or that text, or where the truth lies in the argument, for example, between MPs and MCs. But there are some things we are infallibly certain about, things we state in our confession of faith, when we recite the Apostles' creed or the Nicene creed, for example. If we are not certain of them, then we cannot really say that we are Christians. Well, an infallible papal statement states that kind of faith.

Another point to notice: the Church's infallibility mentioned here (which is the container and measure of papal infallibility) is only engaged where it is a question of the *definition* of doctrine. 'Definition' is a precise term; it does not cover teaching in general, or preaching, or theological exposition, or catechetics. It means the making of a formal—and limiting—*judgement*, in this case of course a *final* judgement from which there can be no appeal. I think there is a real and valuable analogy here in what was said in chapter 3 (Dz 3063) about the pope being the judge of last resort in ecclesiastical cases, from whose court there can be no appeal. And just as a consequence of that was that he should never, in the normal course of things, deliver judgement in the first instance, so here a consequence of his unique participation in the Church's infallibility in defining doctrine is that he should never in the normal course of things step in first to define a doctrine. So far from providing us with infallible pronouncements every morning at the breakfast table with our newspapers, his responsibility is only to define doctrines that are already ripe for defining in the faith of the Church.

Because it is a matter of infallibility in defining doctrine, which is to say making a judgement about it, I think it would have been more accurate to head this chapter 'On the Roman Pontiff's infallible *judicium*', rather than on his 'infallible *magisterium*'.

In the light of these considerations we can also interpret the last statement of the definition: 'and therefore such definitions of the Roman Pontiff are irreformable of themselves, and not as a result of the consent of the Church'. This sentence was added at the last minute, as an afterthought. It might be called the final defiant flourish of ultramontane victory over Gallicanism. But all it really means is that as the supreme representative of the Church the pope has the last word in the definition of doctrine, just as he does in canonical judgements. Since he has the last word it behoves him, as a good chairman of the college of bishops and of the whole ecclesial body, to be extremely chary about uttering the first word.

Let us go on to look at the conditions for the pope to define something infallibly. They are basically two: a condition about how or when he speaks, and a condition about what he speaks of. He can only be sure of speaking infallibly when he speaks *ex cathedra*, which means 'from the throne'—the throne or chair of Peter. This is, of course, a metaphor; but it is a metaphor that one rather expects to see ritually enacted. We are, after all, speaking about an extremely solemn and serious act, the definition of a doctrine of faith, an act about which there should be no doubt; an act about which there *was* no doubt in the definition of the doctrine of the Immaculate Conception in 1854, or of the Assumption in 1950—occasions when, I presume, the pope did take his seat formally upon his *cathedra*. But what the metaphor or symbol means is stated in the next phrase—it represents the pope's apostolic, that is to say his Petrine, authority. So that has to be consciously and deliberately engaged or invoked when he defines infallibly. He also has to be deliberately speaking *ex cathedra* 'as pastor and teacher of all Christians'.

But again, it is not just a matter of his *teaching* as pastor and teacher of all Christians. The pope's infallibility is not engaged when he issues an encyclical on any topic of the day, more or less

controversial, more or less urgent, whether on social justice or
sexual morality or the Holy Spirit or war and peace. It can only be
engaged when he *defines* something, when he deliberately utters
the last word on some point of doctrine. The MP obsession of
'creeping infallibility', which would see infallibility (and hence,
remember, irreformability) in every papal encyclical, in every
papal utterance at every papal audience, in every document to
which the papal signature is attached, is utterly against the true
drift of the 1870 definition. The pope has to be deliberately,
formally solemnly and explicitly *defining* some doctrine of faith
for his charism of infallibility to be engaged. If a papal utterance is
not explicitly, solemnly and formally infallible, then it is not
infallible. It's as simple as that. The definitions of 1854 and 1950
met these requirements; it is hard to think of any other papal
utterances, other than the formal ratification of conciliar definitions, that have done so. As a last resort, as a final guarantee or
assurance of truth, the papal charism of infallibility is indeed
something only very rarely to be invoked.

Coming to the condition limiting the subject to which papal
infallibility applies, we find, to paraphrase, that it is limited to the
field of revealed truth; to the matter of 'faith and morals'. So
whatever the pope (or Church councils for that matter—the
pope's infallibility is no more or no less than the Church's infallibility) may say about history, as in the fifth paragraph of this
chapter of *Pastor Aeternus* which I have characterised as ultramontane myth, or about science, or politics or economics, cannot be
regarded as infallible. Whatever does not fall under the assent of
Christian faith cannot be regarded as an infallible judgement
within the terms of this definition.

A point of difficulty I have about this definition is the inclusion
of 'morals' within the scope of infallible definitions. It is obvious
why it is included; a very great deal of Christian revelation and
doctrine has to do with moral behaviour—the ten commandments, the twin commandments of love, the beatitudes, the ex-
hortations in Paul's letters, and much else. I am not objecting to
the inclusion, but only wondering what an infallible definition
about morals would be like. For according to Thomas Aquinas,[8]
and indeed our common experience, the ultimate judgement
about right or wrong in human behaviour is a judgement about
particular actions. The ultimate judgement is not, for example, 'it
is wrong to kill innocent human beings', but 'It will be wrong for
me, in this particular instance, to kill So-and-so', or 'It was wrong

of you, in this particular case, to kill So-and-so'. Now clearly it is impossible, or at least totally fruitless, for the pope to make infallible definitions about the particular acts of particular persons in particular instances. His infallible moral definitions would have to be more general than that. But is it, in the case of a moral judgement, possible to make a general judgement that will always be true without exception? All we can say is that a definition about morals can be true, and hence infallibly true, in the same way that any statement about morals can be true, which is a way that must allow for exceptions.

NOTES

1 An excellent book for background reading on Vatican I is Abbot Cuthbert Butler's account of it: *The Vatican Council* (2 vols, Longmans, Green, London, 1930).

2 All I have to hand is the text of the Constitution as given in the latest edition of Denzinger's *Enchiridion*. But in any case, this book is not the place for a detailed examination of the history of the text, from the original draft to its final form. I think such an examination would support my observations, but about that there could be differences of opinion.

3 To cite one trivial and one more serious example. Alcoholics who have been cured of their addiction have to abstain totally from alcohol, or their trouble returns. So priests who are alcoholics cannot, with safety to their health and well-being, celebrate mass with alcoholic wine. Now it was established centuries ago by ecclesiastical custom that in case of necessity mass may be validly celebrated with unfermented grape juice. So a priest who is an alcoholic can validly celebrate mass with grape juice. The obvious authority to authorise him to do so is his bishop. But in current practice the bishop may not do so; he has to refer the case to the Holy See, and the necessary permission lies there within the discretion of the Congregation for the Doctrine of the Faith.

The more serious example concerns Greek- and Slavonic-rite Catholics in North America. The traditional canon law of these Churches sanctions the ordination of married men to the priesthood. But the Holy See forbids the emigrant Uniate Churches in North America (and South America too, I imagine) to exercise this right, because it would 'scandalise' the Latin Catholics who are in the majority in those regions.

4 Liberius was one of the many bishops who were exiled by the emperor Constantius in the course of the long-drawn-out wrangles over Arianism and semi-Arianism that followed the Council of Nicaea in 325. The hero of orthodoxy in all these years was St Athanasius of Alexandria. Now

Liberius under pressure did two things that were hardly in accord with the strictest orthodoxy: in the year 357 he excommunicated Athanasius, and subscribed to the semi-Arian creed of the first Council of Sirmium.

Vigilius had an even more unhappy time of it. He was caught up in the obscure and highly ambiguous theological intrigues of the Emperor Justinian, held a prisoner in Constantinople, where he was forced to subscribe to that Emperor's dubious theological formulations, which were aimed at conciliating the Monophysites, and to underwrite the very ambiguous propositions of Constantinople II, which Justinian convoked in 553. However, as that Council has been traditionally accepted as the fifth ecumenical Council by both East and West, I suppose Vigilius' orthodoxy may be said to remain untarnished.

Honorius I offers the clearest instance of a pope straying from the orthodox path. Once more an emperor was trying to find a formula to conciliate the Monophysite Churches, in schism since Chalcedon in 451. This time he got the patriarch of Constantinople, Sergius, to work out two doctrines in succession, the first known as monoenergism, the second as monothelism, which mean respectively attributing only one activity and one will to Christ. Honorius went along with Sergius in this. The doctrines, and both hierarchs, were condemned at Constantinople III, the sixth ecumenical council, in 680.

The following clerihews may help the reader to remember the other-wise not very memorable:

> Poor Pope Honorius
> (625–638) has become rather notorious
> for his inability
> to live up to the requirements of papal infallibility.

> But the case of Pope Liberius
> (352–366) is not nearly so serious;
> although he signed on the wrong dotted line,
> he said afterwards he didn't really mean it, so that's fine.

> As for the wretched Pope Vigilius
> (537–555), he should never have been quite so silly as
> to try to keep up with every current opinion
> of the Emperor Justinian.

5 See the book by Brian Tierney, *The Origins of Papal Infallibility, 1150–1350* (Leiden, 1972), especially pp. 186–196.
6 With Newman, Ward had been one of the leading spirits of the Oxford movement in the Church of England, and he became a Catholic shortly after Newman in the 1840s. Being married, he could not be ordained priest in the Catholic Church, but as a layman he taught theology for many years at the Catholic seminary at Ware. I cannot quote the author-ity for this story about infallible pronouncements every morning for breakfast. It may well be apocryphal.

7 I remember when I was newly arrived in South Africa in 1966, I was asked by the chaplain to Catholic students at the University of Cape Town, a Dominican confrère of mine now gone to his reward, to give a talk on the chief Marian doctrines of the Catholic Church. During the discussion afterwards he himself put a question, or made a point, in which he talked about the dogma 'newly revealed in 1854'. I was unable to persuade him that it was not revealed then, only defined. The feast of the Immaculate Conception was in fact already being celebrated in England in the eleventh century, before the Norman conquest.

8 *Summa Theologiae* Ia IIae, 6, prol.: 'Because activities and operations deal with single objects, it follows that every form of operational knowledge (e.g. mechanics or engineering—or morals) finds its completion in the consideration of particulars. So moral reflections, which are about human activities, must first be set out in general terms, and then get down to particulars'. This is admittedly a very free rendering.

8

LUMEN GENTIUM, 1964:
A CRITICAL EXAMINATION*

One has to admit, ruefully but realistically, that Vatican II's dogmatic Constitution De Ecclesia, *Lumen Gentium*, is not quite the ministerial collegialist charter we MCs would like to claim it for. And indeed, after nine hundred years of the relentlessly advancing tide of magisterial papalism, that is hardly surprising. The years between 1870 and 1958 (the death of Pius XII) saw that movement reach its spring tide high water mark. John XXIII and the Council he convoked represent the beginning of the ebb. It has been rather absurdly utopian of many of us to have expected the waters to recede in a tide race; in many important channels, as we have found by experience, particularly in this decade of the 80s, they are still coming in on the flood. Nevertheless, with *Lumen Gentium* (and other Council documents) the tide has definitely turned. A glance at the history of this Constitution will demonstrate this. After this glance we shall look more closely at its treatment of themes that have commanded our attention in this book—Church universal and local Churches; ecumenism; collegiality; authority as service; hierarchy and priesthood; *magisterium*.

A. History of the document

The draft schema drawn up by the preparatory commission and presented at the first session of the Council in 1962, was a document of eleven chapters (AS I, iv, pp. 12–91). Chapters 1 and 2 dealt with the nature of the Church militant, its membership and the necessity of it for salvation. Chapters 3 and 4 dealt with the

* (For this chapter I have had access to the *Acta Synodalia Sacrosancti Concilii Oecumenici Vaticani II*, in several massive volumes. In what follows they are referred to as AS.)

episcopate and priesthood (*sacerdotium*) and with residential bishops, one brief paragraph being given to their 'collegiality'. Chapter 5 was devoted to the states of perfection (religious life), chapter 6 to the laity, chapter 7 to the Church's *magisterium*, chapter 8 to authority and obedience in the Church, chapter 9 to relations between Church and State, chapter 10 to the Church's obligation to proclaim the gospel to all nations everywhere, and chapter 11 to ecumenism (wholly misunderstood, but we shall return to that later).

The document is drawn up from a purely ultramontane MP point of view, in spite of a few nods in the direction of some concepts being thrown up by contemporary theology, like collegiality, ecumenism and the priesthood of all the faithful. It strikes me as presenting a papalism developed from the basis of Vatican I, 1870—a papalism, therefore, even more extreme than the ultramontanism that triumphed then. I have not been able to compare it with the schema *De Ecclesia Christi* that was prepared for Vatican I; but it would not surprise me if this first schema presented to Vatican II proved to be much the more narrowly ultramontane and unbalanced of the two.

It was criticised very severely in the debate at the first session. We shall look in detail at some of the criticisms when we consider how *Lumen Gentium* treats the themes we have listed. Here I will just note the crucial intervention of Bishop De Smedt of Bruges (AS I, iv, pp. 142–143), who accused the document of the famous three vices of triumphalism, clericalism and juridicism (which is not quite the same thing as what we usually mean by legalism); also those of Cardinals Frings (Cologne) and Bea (*ibid.*, pp. 218–219, 229), who pointed out that the 'tradition' on which the document drew in support of its propositions was almost entirely that of the last hundred years—make it two hundred to be generous.

The net result was that the document was referred to a reconstituted theological commission to be entirely redrafted in the light of criticisms and suggestions made in the debate, or to be submitted in writing. So at the second session, which opened in September 1963 (after the death of John XXIII and the election of Paul VI), a new draft was submitted, of only four chapters (AS II, i, 215–281). It began with a chapter on the mystery of the Church, went on in chapter 2 to 'the hierarchical constitution of the Church, and specifically the episcopate', in chapter 3 to 'the people of God and specifically the laity', and in chapter 4 to 'the vocation to holiness

in the Church'—a much wider perspective than the corresponding states of perfection (chapter 5) of the first schema. These were
the only chapters presented and discussed in the second session;
others reappeared in the final draft (AS III, iv, pp. 158–374), the
fruit of second-session debates and suggestions, which was
presented to the third session, in 1964, as follows:

chapter 1	The Mystery of the Church
chapter 2	The People of God
chapter 3	The hierarchical constitution of the Church, and specifically the episcopate
chapter 4	The laity
chapter 5	The universal call to holiness in the Church
chapter 6	Religious
chapter 7	The eschatological essence of our calling and our union with the heavenly Church
chapter 8	The blessed Virgin Mary Mother of God in the mystery of Christ and of the Church.

With all its eventual emendations this document was approved by
2,134 votes to 10 on 19 November 1964.

A few general observations before we go on to consider our
selected themes in detail. The triumphalism Bishop De Smedt
complained of has been almost eliminated, the juridicism much
reduced, and the clericalism mitigated. The Church is first
viewed as a mystery or 'sacrament' as it is called in the first
paragraph, rather than as a juridical structure; the episcopate is to
some extent subordinated to the people of God it is instituted to
serve; the laity, also to some extent, are brought in from the
fringes of the institution a little closer to the heart of the mystery.
In the debate on the first schema Archbishop Lefebvre (who has
since totally renounced Vatican II and all its works and all its
pomps) proposed that there should be two conciliar statements on
the Church, one dogmatic, in formal technical language, for the
benefit of theologians and seminary professors, the other pastoral, in simple language, for ordinary Catholics (AS I, iv, pp.
144ff.). His suggestion was followed to this extent that it was
decided also to draw up the Constitution on the Church in the
modern world, *Gaudium et Spes*. It is not within the scope of this

book to discuss any other Vatican II documents, but it is fair to observe that *Gaudium et Spes*, and the decrees on ecumenism, laity, missions and religious freedom in particular provide a wider, more catholic context for *Lumen Gentium* than was ever envisaged by the drafters of the first schema.

B. 'Church' and 'Churches'

One of the main theological bases of the MC party—or that segment of it to which I adhere—is the priority in the concrete existential order of the local Church over the universal Church. We think there should be much less talk about the Catholic Church, and much more talk about the Catholic Churches. The primary references of the word 'Church' when it is used in the universal sense should be to the mystery, the idea, the heavenly reality, and not to the Church as a world-wide institution. What we have world-wide in the order of concrete institution—or what we should perceive ourselves as having—is a great number of local Churches, each embodying and representing in its own place the one, holy, catholic and apostolic Church (the mystery), and united with each other in one communion under the presidency of the local Church of Rome and the primacy of its bishop. I have to admit that this is not the basic theological stance of *Lumen Gentium*, though it is not ruled out by it. *Lumen Gentium* starts indeed with the Church as a mystery, but as soon as it translates the mystery into the existential or institutional order, it translates it into the world-wide institution of the Roman Catholic Church, and as it were derives local Churches from this Church universal.

In fact on this theme its point of view differs little if at all from that of the original schema. That document explicitly declares local Churches to be formed on the model (*ad imaginem*) of the universal Church (cap. 4, 15: AS I, iv, p. 26). *Lumen Gentium* echoes this bad theology in 3, 23; but in 3, 26 it does suggest that the local Church embodies the universal Church, instead of just forming a part of it and being modelled on it. The passage is worth quoting in full, because in spite of my earlier pessimism it does go some way to substantiate the MC theology sketched in the previous paragraph:

> This Church of Christ is truly present in all legitimate local gatherings of the faithful, which . . . are themselves called

Churches in the new testament. For these are in their own
localities the new People called by God 'in the Holy Spirit
and in much fulness' (1 Thess 1:5) . . . In these communities,
though often small and poor, or residing in 'the diaspora',
Christ is present whose power gathers together the one,
holy, catholic and apostolic Church. Indeed 'sharing in the
body and blood of Christ has precisely the effect of trans-
forming us into what we receive' (Leo the Great, *Sermon* 63,
7: PL 54, 357D).

Perhaps significantly, *Lumen Gentium* does not incorporate a
quotation that the original schema puts in from Basil the Great (*in
Isaiam*, 15, 296: PG 30, 637), in which he says the mystical body is
a body of Churches (AS 1, iv, p. 27). For this does imply that local
Churches are parts of the body, parts of the universal Church, as
counties are parts of the United Kingdom, or states parts of the
United States. The important ideas of embodiment and representation are absent.

The debates and written memoranda on the second draft of the
Constitution during the second session in 1963 produced some
interesting proposals, one of which was mostly incorporated in
the final document, the other two regrettably not. Anthony
Grauls, Archbishop of Kitega in Burundi, speaking in the name of
fifty-five bishops of central Africa, wanted something much
more definite said about the *catholicity* of the Church, as distinct
from its unity. He implied that these two notes of the Church are
in tension with each other, something that is rarely remarked on.
It is rather ironic that in the Catholic Church, at least within its
overwhelmingly dominant Latin tradition, it is unity rather than
catholicity that has preoccupied the minds of theologians and
authorities alike—unity best promoted, it has been assumed, by a
constant encouragement of uniformity in rite and centralisation in
government. The African bishops make it quite clear that catholicity means *diversity*, and pluriformity rather than uniformity
among Churches. Thus their spokesman says: ' . . . the Church
tends towards unity in diversity and diversity in unity. Hence the
legitimacy is clear, within the ecclesiastical communion, of Churches which enjoy their own proper traditions, liturgies and forms
of government' (AS II, ii, p. 69; also p. 161).

To meet this incontrovertible point a whole new paragraph
(13) was added to chapter 2 of *Lumen Gentium* on the people of
God. It is not quite so strong on the positive value of diversity,

not quite so emphatic against uniformity as I (or, I am sure, the bishops of central Africa) would have liked; there still creeps in a suggestion that diversity is *dangerous* to unity, the obsessive ultramontane preoccupation. All this, presumably, because of a rearguard action of MPs in the theological commission. It is thus very interesting to find in the *relatio*, or explanatory note on this paragraph, the statement that 'Subcommission II decided to satisfy these desires by introducing several elements into the text before you, in the following way: 1 . . . 2 . . . 3. This universality or catholicity rejects (*respuit*, 'spits out') uniformity: it preserves diversity in unity by procuring communion and co-operation between the diverse peoples and diverse orders in the Church' (AS III, i, p. 201). The final text, however, says nothing about 'spitting out uniformity', or even preserving diversity in unity; it talks rather of the see of Peter protecting legitimate varieties, and 'being vigilant that particularities do not harm unity in any way, but rather serve its interests'. Precisely the opposite emphasis to the one 'decided on' by Subcommission II; it is again unity, not catholicity, that is the object of primary anxiety.

The idea of the institutional priority of local Churches over the universal Church (as institution) is most intimately connected with the concept of collegiality. Both concepts were very close to the hearts of the bishops of the oriental Churches at the Council. The proposal I come to next was formally a proposal on collegiality, but I treat it here because of its obvious bearing on the theme of local Churches over against the universal Church. It was put forward by Bishop Isaac Ghattas of Thebes, in Egypt. It is too long to put here, but so good that I give a translation of the whole of it in Appendix 2. It is worth noting in passing, that the oriental bishops, in order to make the point that the Catholic Church is not identical with the Latin Church, refused on principle to speak Latin at the Council or submit their written proposals in Latin. It would have been unrealistic for them to make their contributions in Coptic or Greek, in Syriac, Armenian or Church Slavonic—so they normally spoke and wrote in French.[1]

Bishop Ghattas proposes scrapping chapters 2 and 3 of the original draft, on the episcopate and residential bishops, and replacing it with the text he offers (Appendix 2, p. 137; AS II, i, pp. 525f.). In some ways it is a little utopian and unrealistic. But its great merit is that it proposes to *institutionalise* collegiality and the theology of local Churches. These ideas, Bishop Ghattas says very realistically, must be practised as well as recognised 'in order to quieten the fears of our Orthodox brethren' (note the ecumenical concern), 'and concretely to open our doors to them'. And to be practised they have to be given institutional or canonical embodiment. This is something the enormous Latin majority at the Council does not seem to have appreciated, not even the dominant majority of moderate MCs. They had all been brought up on the Code of Canon Law, promulgated by the Holy See in 1917, and on the juridically dubious assumption that legislating, or making canon law is a prerogative of the Holy See. So instead of a realistically rewritten version of Bishop Ghattas' proposal, what we get is chapter 3 of *Lumen Gentium*, which certainly says a number of good things about the authority of bishops, and its being essentially a service, and about collegiality, and about local Churches, but does nothing to give these beautiful ideas sharp canonical institutional teeth. The minority MP party was of course delighted. It benefited from that abhorrence of juridicism voiced by Bishop De Smedt. It is very proper to abhor the influence of juridicism on dogma and theology; but to carry this abhorrence to the point of shrinking from making any rules or laws or canons is not wise. It is really rather ironical that a council summoned as pre-eminently a pastoral council should have enacted no legislation at all, and should have left that 'chore' to the Holy See. Legislation left to the Holy See means legislation left in the control of the MP party which is dominant in the Roman curia.

It is not surprising, then, that one of the suggestions made by a Spanish bishop, Fidel García Martínez, failed to get into the final document—and failed, what is more, to influence the New Code of Canon Law, promulgated in 1983. To a short spoken intervention on the subject of infallibility he added written observations of a quite inordinate length—which is perhaps why they were for the most part ignored. On the *practical* implementation of collegiality, he observes first that norms currently restricting the exercise of episcopal authority were hardly justified by pastoral requirements, which vary so enormously from one region of the world to another; and secondly and most urgently that the current centralised practice of the Holy See appointing almost all bishops of the Latin Church (a practice made into 'the norm' in the New Code, though it is in fact canonically a very recent innovation) is of very dubious pastoral value. He tends to favour a system of co-option by the other bishops of a province or region (AS II, ii, p. 112). There are of course other possibilities, and there is no reason why there should be one system of selecting bishops for the whole world. Bishop García, for all his long-windedness, had the merit of pointing out that the present system is unsatisfactory, and the whole question is urgent—and the Council simply sidestepped the question. He was, after all, only an auxiliary bishop.

To sum up, the Council did in the realm of theory do something to open the way to a sounder theology of local Churches, and to that extent I must correct the pessimism of my opening paragraph. But *practically* speaking, it did nothing to change the situation prevailing before the Council, and so in practical terms nothing has changed to this very day.[2]

C.   Collegiality

Collegiality is so closely connected to the theme of local Churches—perhaps as unity to catholicity—that it is right to deal with it next.

We begin with the brief statement of collegiality, so meagre as to be in effect false, to be found in the original schema at the end of chapter 4 on residential bishops, paragraph 16. Here it is in full:

> (*The College of Bishops*). The College of Bishops, which is the successor of the College of Apostles in *magisterium* and pastoral government, in which indeed the College of Apostles permanently persists and in which permanent witness is borne to the mission of Christ and his teaching and laws, together with its head the Roman Pontiff and never without this head, is held to be one subject of full and supreme authority over the universal Church. The authority of this College, however, even though it is ordinary as inhering in it *ex officio*, nonetheless is only lawfully exercised in an extraordinary manner and in devout subordination to the Vicar of Jesus Christ on earth, when, how and as long as it seems expedient to him in the Lord. As regards the constitution of this august College, all residential Bishops living at peace with the Apostolic See are members of it by right, and none of the Bishops, whether residential or otherwise can belong to this College unless he has been taken into it by the express act or at least the tacit consent of the successor of Peter, Christ's Vicar and Head of the College (AS I, iv, p. 27).

This extraordinary paragraph in effect identifies the college of bishops with an ecumenical council, and rather contemptuously (calling it 'august' merely rubs salt in the wound) makes it a mere instrument of the Holy See, to be employed at papal pleasure. Fortunately it disappeared almost without trace from the revised schema presented to the second session in September 1963. The eventual chapter 3, on the hierarchical constitution of the Church and specifically on the episcopate, elaborates the concept of collegiality much more positively and less grudgingly in two long sections, 22 and 23, with further implications drawn in 25. One can in fact say that after Vatican II the notion of collegiality must enter integrally into any genuine Catholic doctrine of the episcopate, and hence of the sacrament of order.

It was, however, one of the teachings of the Council to which the MP curial party put up the most stubborn resistance. For them, with their very narrow notion of authority, collegiality constitutes a serious threat to papal primacy—whereas in fact all that it really threatens is papal absolutism and excessive curial centralisation. I think there can be little doubt that the Roman curia is neurotically obsessed with the matter of papal authority. And so insistently were these neurotic fears expressed at the Council, that they found their way into the final text. In the three sections of chapter 3 that I mentioned above, which are dealing *ex professo* with the episcopate and its collegial structure, and not with the papal primacy and infallibility, which were adequately defined, surely, in 1870, there are no less than twelve references to the special position and authority of the Roman pontiff, where one only at the very beginning would have been sufficient, stating that he is the head of the episcopal college, and that the authority of the college in no way derogates from the *plena potestas* of the papal office. It is impossible not to sense the note of obsessive anxiety that motivates these tedious and unnecessary references.

But let me quote in support some of the Council Fathers themselves, because naturally I am suspect of having my own little obsession about magisterial papalism. Some of the most forceful promoters of collegiality, and of the pluriformity, or true catholicity of the Church, were the bishops of the Eastern Churches. Here is the Melkite patriarch of Antioch, Maximus IV Saigh, speaking in the debate on the original schema in December 1962:

> But the unilateral, and thus incomplete aspect of our schema appears above all when it speaks of the primacy of Peter and of his successors. Quite apart from the *sickly insistence* [my emphasis—an English speaker would probably have said a

'neurotic insistence']³ on repeating this truth, as if the whole of Christianity were contained in this dogma, the text isolates the Roman Pontiff from the rest of the hierarchy, as if in the Church there was only the pope to represent Christ, and the flock of subordinates who are subjected to him . . . I have only wished to give some examples of this unilateralness (I should say: of this partiality) with which a certain school treats theological problems, to the extent of distorting them, ending up by accusing ecumenism of wishing to water down the truth and to seek compromises in the faith. Such compromises nobody wants, neither Catholic ecumenists, nor our Orthodox and Protestant brothers (AS I, iv, p. 296).

I have lengthened the quotation to include the remark on ecumenism, though it is not strictly to our present point, so that I can simply refer back to it when we come to the theme of ecumenism. But the whole speech, and particularly this section of it, is to my mind a damning indictment of the whole MP mentality.

Coming to the debate ten months later or so on the redrafted schema in 1963, we have the same complaint made, this time by Cardinal Frings of Cologne:

In the chapter on the hierarchical constitution of the Church and on the bishops many beautiful things are said about ecclesiastical offices as functions of service, not of dominion; about the college of bishops under its head, the supreme pontiff. But in the article which treats of the bishops' office of teaching, more is said about the office of the supreme pontiff and his infallibility than about the bishops' office of teaching, to the extent that one perceives a certain anxiety, as though by giving more emphasis to the authority of bishops one could somehow detract from the authority of the supreme pontiff. What Pope Gregory the Great did should be taken as an example in this matter, when he wrote to Eulogius patriarch of Alexandria that it was not right for him to be called universal pope, which Eulogius had done, and he supports his judgement with those splendid words quoted by Vatican I . . . (AS II, i, p. 344).

It is most gratifying to find Cardinal Frings also drawing attention to the *context* of the quotation from Gregory the Great. I am sure he would approve of my including the whole letter in this book as Appendix 1.

He is supported in the same debate by the Archbishop of Saragossa, Casimir Morcillo González, who said that the schema should return to its proper road, from which it had wandered in a number of respects, among them: 'The schema is too repetitive in its proclamation and defence of the primacy of the Roman Pontiff. Not that the doctrine is not true, but that it is not necessary to assert the doctrine again and again' (*ibid.*, p. 352). Bishop Ghattas of Thebes in Egypt, whom we quoted in the previous section, makes the same point.

Back to the first session and the debate on the original schema, for a little gem from the Maronite Bishop Michael Doumith, who did, as a matter of fact, speak in Latin. He remarks: 'When episcopal authority is being described, frequent warnings are given to use this authority well, and also frequent reminders of the primacy of the Roman Pontiff, from which this authority depends—like a mother who gives her little boy a toy and is afraid he will break it' (AS I, iv, p. 255). But none of this gentle mockery could alleviate the fears of the curial MP Fathers, and so they were allowed to disfigure the final document and somewhat emasculate the doctrine, and above all the practice of genuine collegiality. Again, as we remarked at the end of the previous section, it was a failure of the Council, which the MPs undoubtedly welcomed and to some extent contrived, not to provide collegiality with any institutional embodiment, but to leave such practicalities to the Holy See. So after the Council Paul VI set up the triennial synod of bishops as really not much more than an august talking shop. And in the last year or so Cardinal Ratzinger (who to a very considerable extent speaks for the Holy See) has been doing his best to play down the authority of bishops' conferences. The proposers and supporters of collegiality were naïve enough to hand over its implementations to its most committed opponents, who, being anything but naïve, have done their best to neutralise it ever since.

D. Ecumenism

Ecumenism was undoubtedly one of the successes of the Council. There had, as we can gather from the speech of Maximus IV Saigh, been Catholic ecumenists at work before the Council. We have already met one of the most eminent of them in the previous chapter, Dom Lambert Beauduin, OSB. One of the staunchest of them in England was my much revered confrère Fr Henry St John, OP. But they were not generally approved of, or understood either by the ecclesiastical authorities or by the Catholic public at large. How little they were understood or approved of by curial MP theologians may be seen by the chapter on ecumenism in the original schema *De Ecclesia*.

It begins by lamenting 'the separations from the Catholic Church' that have occurred through the centuries, which obscure its 'indefectible unity', and declares that the Council says nothing must be left undone to restore the integral unity of all Christians, 'all the more urgently since by the disposition of divine providence the separated communities of Christians are themselves also aspiring to the unity of all'. What it clearly has in mind is the 'return' of these communities to the bosom of the Catholic Church. In a subsequent paragraph indeed it goes on to say 'The Catholic Church regards all separated Christians with maternal charity, and lovingly invites them to herself'. It will always be a question of separated Christians 'acceding to the unity of the Church', whether as individuals or as communities. In a word, the chapter reaffirms what was the common doctrine, that the Catholic Church is the only true Church, that it has maintained and other communities (they are never here called Churches) have lost the essential unity of the Church Christ founded, that it alone has been entrusted with the fullness of revelation, and so that is where all Christians have to acknowledge it to be. The ecumenical movement outside the Catholic Church is welcomed, and informed that of necessity it must lead those 'who intend to obey the will of Christ with their whole heart and to grow in the grade of "ecumenicity", under the guidance of the Holy Spirit, to accede more and more to that Church which, although it is the one and indivisible house of God, nevertheless rejoices in many mansions in the whole world, in unity of faith, government and communion under the one Vicar of Christ'.

The ecumenical movement within the Catholic Church is also welcomed, and told that its work is to strive theologically and pastorally to show all Christians more and more clearly that the Church is their paternal home, and to help the separated communities find their way to true unity all the more easily. It is then warned of the prudence needed to avoid indifferentism and interconfessionalism. The old prohibition of any *communicatio in sacris* is then renewed at some length, and Catholics are told they may, however, co-operate in social and economic good works, provided certain precautions are taken so that this can 'happen without spiritual danger' (AS I, iv, pp. 81–87).

It was enough to make any genuine ecumenist's hair stand on end. What was missing from the narrow, rigid and 'triumphalist' ecclesiology that lay behind this stand, was any sense of the deficiencies, historically verifiable, in the Catholic Church's (*in concreto* the Latin Church's) appropriation of the revelation it had been entrusted with; it may never have formally taught falsehood, but it has certainly often failed to teach all the truth, and in its policies at times has condoned or even encouraged attitudes and prejudices at variance with the gospel. That the Catholic (*in concreto* the Latin) Church may have much, if not to learn, at least to be *reminded of* by the 'separated communities'—this was never for a moment envisaged by the drafters of this chapter.

Well, mercifully, 'by the guidance of the Holy Spirit', the whole chapter was scrapped, and a separate decree of the Council, still not perfect and evincing certain timidities, but all the same far more positive and encouraging, was devoted to the subject. And above all, before the final session of the Council Paul VI gave a definitive statute and status to the Secretariat for Christian Unity under Cardinal Bea. Ecumenism was at last respectable.

With that decree we cannot deal here. How the change took place from the original chapter seems to me something of a miracle. That that chapter represented the common Catholic viewpoint, certainly the common viewpoint of English Catholics, is suggested by the intervention of Cardinal Godfrey of Westminster in the first session (AS I, iv, pp. 221f.) and of his successor Archbishop Heenan in the second (AS II, ii, pp. 52f.), who spoke in the name of all the bishops of England and Wales. Both were clearly still thinking in terms of 'the conversion of England—and Wales', which we all used earnestly to pray for in those days; meaning the conversion of our Protestant friends of all denominations (we didn't think the differences between them really mattered very much) to the Roman Catholic Church and Roman Catholic religion as it was lived and practised and believed then and there. The second intervention, that of Archbishop Heenan, was on what is now paragraph 15 of chapter 2 of *Lumen Gentium*, and it is fairly clear that he and his colleagues did not really understand the intention of this section of that chapter on the people of God—which was in fact to state that others besides Catholics may well in fact belong to the people of God in one way or another. The proposal they made was not accepted.

On the other hand, there was another voice from England, that of Abbot Christopher Butler, OSB, president of the English Benedictine Congregation, speaking about the same paragraph as Archbishop Heenan. He wanted a definite statement inserted about what later came to be called the ecclesiality of the 'separated communities', that is to say that they are not 'merely natural societies or communities' (AS II, i, p. 262). His full proposal was not included either in the final text; but it would talk about baptised Christians 'who recognise and receive other sacraments also in their own Churches or ecclesiastical communities'.

But my impression is (or should I say my guess, since I have not studied the records of the debates in detail) that it was the missionary bishops and those of the Eastern Churches who provided the main impulse to what can justly be called the ecumenical revolution at Vatican II. We have already noted the words of Patriarch Maximus IV Saigh on the topic, and those of Bishop Ghattas. There was also a charming, and I imagine effective, intervention from Bishop van Cauwelaert, bishop of Inongo in Congo-Léopoldville as it then was. He said:

> In vain do we teach that the Catholic Church is the true Church of Christ . . . , if the honest features of Christian brotherhood cannot be discerned in its life . . . So we ought to show that the Church's task is to actuate the primitive idea of the Jerusalem Church . . . where the multitude of believers was of one mind and heart . . . Then, without any injurious invocation of law, we shall be able to preach to those who are living outside the Church the need to enter the Church to find salvation, because then the Church will present them with the idea of unity and fraternity . . . This message will so move our African peoples that they will no longer be able to resist it, since they are wearied of western domination and are seeking the brotherhood of the great family of nations . . . Then also we shall be able to invite our brothers from Protestantism, not to submit themselves to some authority whose mission they do not understand, but to co-operate with us in restoring gradually and in charity the unity of one faith (AS I, iv, pp. 157f.).

The net result of such interventions was a tiny change in the final draft of *Lumen Gentium* which made possible (I would indeed say mandatory) a more open and genial Catholic ecclesiology in which a genuine Catholic ecumenism could have free rein. We are in chapter I, which has been talking about the mystery of the

Church, and the various figures and images employed to convey it in the New Testament. Paragraph 8, headed 'On the Church, at once visible and spiritual', states the identity of this mystery with the empirical Catholic Church we all know here and now. The text of the second draft, 1963, ran:

> This Church, therefore, true Mother and Mistress of all, established and organised in this world as a society, *is* the Catholic Church, directed by the Roman Pontiff and the Bishops in communion with him, although outside its total structure several elements of sanctification can be found, which as things proper to the Church of Christ conduce to Catholic unity (AS III, i, pp. 167f.).

The final text of *Lumen Gentium*, as submitted to the third session of the Council in 1964 and there approved, runs:

> This Church, established and organised in this world as a society, *subsists in* the Catholic Church, governed by the successor of Peter and the Bishops in communion with him, although outside its structure several elements of sanctification and truth are to be found, which as gifts proper to the Church conduce to Catholic unity.

The only alteration I wish to consider is that of 'is' to 'subsists in', though the substitution of 'successor of Peter' for 'Roman Pontiff', and the addition of 'and of truth' to 'elements of sanctification', are also distinct improvements.

The notes provided by the theological commission to this final draft do not attribute 'subsists in' to any suggestion made by any of the Fathers. They simply state, 'instead of "is" it says "subsists in"', as an expression more in harmony with the affirmation of ecclesial elements which are present elsewhere' (AS III, i, p. 177). So we must attribute it to the inspiration of some member of the theological commission, or one of the *periti* attached to it.

The significance of this tiny change is in my view overwhelming. What had hitherto rendered Catholic participation in the ecumenical movement almost impossible (because self-contradictory) was the Roman Catholic Church's simple and unqualified identification of itself, and itself alone, with 'the Church Christ founded'. If that is the case, there can be no discussion with 'separated communities' about essentials, about those 'non-negotiables' we wearily hear so much about nowadays in secular conflicts, since such separated communities have no *locus standi* as Church. All that can be discussed is suitable conditions or terms for their 'return to Catholic unity' (there is still a whiff of this attitude in the final phrase of the passage quoted). Now the word 'is' states this simple and unqualified identification *exclusively*: this Church is the Catholic Church; it is not therefore any other so-called 'Church'.

But the phrase 'subsists in', while still affirming the identification, breaks its exclusiveness. Something conceptualised or described can *be* only one concrete reality; it can *subsist* in several, in varying degrees. I picture the 'is' diagram something like this: several separate circles, one of them filled in, the others void; the filled-in one is the Catholic Church, the void ones are the 'separated communities', and the Church Christ founded, the Church described as mystery in paragraphs 1–7 of chapter 1, is only the Catholic Church, not any of the others.

But the 'subsists in' diagram is one of concentric circles; the Catholic Church is the inner circle (none of them are filled in totally), and in it the mystery of the Church subsists to the fullest degree empirically attainable on this earth (which is not complete or perfect), while it also subsists in varying lesser degrees in other Churches and ecclesial communities, which are located on the outer circles, according to the elements of truth and sanctification to be found in them.

Thus such a small change (comparable to the old distinction between *homoousion* and *homoiousion* in the trinitarian wrangles of the fourth century) has in principle introduced a vital element of sanctification and truth into the self-perception of Roman Catholics; we may no longer pride ourselves on belonging to the Church that has a monopoly of truth and knows all the answers, the Church that has nothing to learn from any other body. This is the beginning of a supremely important mental and emotional revolution in the Catholic mind. Just how important, is indicated by the fact that in the last year or two, when the MP backlash in Rome has been at its most energetic, murmurs have been heard from some curial theologians, not too far from the Congregation for the Doctrine of the Faith, to the effect that 'subsists in' means exactly the same as 'is', no more no less, and therefore there has been no change in the traditional basic Catholic ecclesiology. This disservice to the truth, this denial of the crucial change of course, which was initiated, however hesitantly, by *Lumen Gentium* and by Vatican II as a whole, must be resisted to the finish.

E.   Authority as service

It will be recalled from the first section of this chapter that the
original schema presented to the first session of the Council in
1962 had a special chapter (8) devoted to the subject of authority
and obedience in the Church (AS 1, iv, pp. 60–63). It never once
refers to the texts from the gospels which provide chapter 2
of this book with its foundations; the key text for the schema
is Rom 13:1, which it paraphrases as saying that all legitimate
authority is from God. As this is a favourite text of, among
others, the South African government, it will readily be understood that it fails to capture immediately the goodwill of a whole
class of readers—those who regard governments like the South
African as offences in the nostrils of men, crying to heaven for
vengeance.

The chapter does talk about authority in the Church as 'a
humble service bestowed on brethren'. But its only conception of
authority is what I called the centurion's conception—a matter of
'go-and-he-goeth, come-and-he-cometh'. There is a give-away
passage in the section on the right way of exercising this kind of
authority. Persons in authority must set a good example by the
obedience they themselves show to their superiors; they should
provide themselves with suitable advisers; 'indeed they should
not refuse, if it seems opportune in the Lord, in order that they
may form a right judgement, to hear the mind even of their
subjects'.

· The chapter did not survive. It was properly felt sufficient to
have a chapter on the episcopate and the ministry of bishops. This
was chapter 2 of the revised draft presented at the second session
in 1963. One crucial change was proposed, and accepted, in the
debates on this draft: to divide chapter 3, on the people of God and
the laity, and put a distinct chapter on the people of God in front
of the chapter on the bishops. So now, by the very arrangement of
the final text of *Lumen Gentium*, we have the episcopal (and papal)
hierarchy implicitly subordinated, as means to end, to the people
they are designed to serve.

One of the first to propose this change was Bishop Joseph
Gargitter of Brixen; and he went on to remark that some of the
old authority attitudes still lingered on in the revised text. 'There
are several lovely things said in the schema', he remarked, 'about
the people of God; but they are too off-hand (*obiter*), and not
infrequently said in such a way as to remind us with a certain

anxiety (that neurotic touch again) of the dependence of the laity on the hierarchy. This also happens where it is talking about bishops, where again mention is made too frequently of their necessary submission under the authority of the Roman Pontiff' (AS II, i, p. 360).

The final text is not without such blemishes, as we noticed in the preceding section. But it does use the word 'ministry' much more frequently of the episcopal office, and it has these two significant things to say in paragraph 27 of chapter 3, on the bishops' office of governing:

> Bishops rule the Churches committed to them as vicars and delegates of Christ, by advice, persuasion and example, but also by authority and sacred power. This however they only use for building up their flock in truth and holiness, remembering that he who is greater should become like the least, and the leader as one who serves (Lk 22:26–27) . . .

> Let the bishop, sent by the Father of the household to govern his family, hold before his eyes the example of the Good Shepherd, who came not to be served but to serve (Mk 10:45), and to lay down his life for his sheep (Jn 10:11). Taken from men and encompassed with weakness, he can sympathise with those who are ignorant and go astray. He should not refuse to listen to his subjects, whom he cherishes as his true children and urges to collaborate generously with himself.

Paragraph 37 in chapter 4 on the laity has this to say on the matter of the laity making themselves heard. It represents an enormous advance on the original schema's chapter on authority and obedience, and places a stricter obligation, I think, on bishops than the passage just quoted would suggest:

> The laity have the right . . . to make known to their sacred pastors their needs and wishes with the freedom and confidence that befits children of God and brothers in Christ. In proportion to the knowledge, the competence and the distinction they enjoy, they have the right (*facultas*) and sometimes even the duty of expressing their opinion on matters affecting the good of the Church. This should be done, where possible, through the institutions established by the Church for the purpose, and always with truth, frankness and prudence, and with respect and love towards those who by virtue of their sacred office represent Christ.

I must point out that the translation of this passage in the Walter M. Abbott edition of the *Documents of Vatican II* is very unsatisfactory and conveys quite the wrong impression.

A note on this final text, as it was presented for discussion at the third session in 1964, makes it clear, as regards 'the institutions established by the Church for the purpose', that at the time of writing there were none! (AS III, i, p. 289, note (F)). It remarks that the question of setting them up belongs rather to a practical decree, and no such decree, as far as I know, issued from Vatican II.

Once again, therefore the Council has put into circulation a coinage of excellent principles; it emphasises that bishops are as much the brothers as the fathers of the laity; that the laity have rights to the services of the bishops (and other clergy); that authority in the Church is not primarily a matter of saying 'Do this' and 'Don't do that', but primarily a matter of serving. And once again it fails to provide even a sketch of the institutions needed to put these principles into effective practice.

Nowhere in the texts, or in the debates, does one find an awareness of the notion of 'responsibility'—I mean what in England we call constitutional responsibility. One of the more obvious things, surely, about the master–servant relationship is that servants are answerable, or responsible, to their masters for their service. We have seen in an earlier chapter how Peter did not question that he was responsible or answerable to the brethren in Jerusalem for his conduct in answering the summons of Cornelius, and so 'going in to uncircumcised men and eating with them'. (Acts 11:2; above, Chapter 2, C.2). So if the notion of authority in the Church as service is to mean anything more than a moral ideal (in that minimal or spiritualised sense MPs also accept it), there need to be institutions, in any society more complex than a face-to-face local group, through which those servants in authority may answer for their authoritative actions to their masters for whose benefit they exercise that authority—in other words, representative institutions which have their own proper authority too. If the pope is genuinely the servant of the servants of God (or slave of the slaves of God, to be pedantic about it), then he should welcome the creation of institutions that enable him to give his masters, who are his brothers and sisters in Christ, an account of his stewardship. And the same, *mutatis mutandis*, for bishops and parish priests.

But the Council took no steps to set up such institutions.

F. Hierarchy and priesthood

It is evident from the text of chapter 3 of *Lumen Gentium* on 'the hierarchical constitution of the Church', that Vatican II was still wedded to the hierarchical concept. The frequent use of the word 'sacred' with reference to the ordained ministry, especially to the bishops, is a further indication of this. What one can say, however, with some relief, is that the hierarchical sacerdotalism which dominated Catholic ecclesiology before the Council has been very considerably mitigated. It would have been wonderful if that chapter had been entitled instead 'on the fraternal constitution of the Church', and rewritten accordingly. This was not to be, but even so the notion of the Church as a brotherhood, and of all its members as basically equal in their membership is given real prominence in the whole Constitution.

In particular, paragraph 32 of chapter 4 on the laity can be taken as a kind of charter of 'equality and fraternity' in the Church. It is a very common mistake to assume that differences among human beings in talents, fortune, culture and so on, and diversity of roles mean and involve inequality—i.e. that people are of unequal worth. This paragraph is an excellent preventative of such a mistake, and is worth reproducing in full:

> (*On the dignity of the laity as members of the People of God*). Holy Church, by divine institution, is set in order and governed with a wonderful variety. 'For just as in one body we have many members, but all the members do not have the same function; so too, being many, we are one body in Christ, each and all of us members one of another' (Rom 12:4–5).
>
> One, therefore, is the chosen People of God; 'one Lord, one faith, one baptism' (Eph 4:5); the members have a common dignity through their regeneration in Christ; a common grace of sonship, a common vocation to perfection, one salvation, one hope and undivided charity. So in Christ and in the Church there is no inequality with respect to race or nationality, social status or sex, because 'there is neither Jew nor Greek; there is neither slave nor free; there is neither male nor female; for you are all "one man" in Christ Jesus' (Gal 3:28, Greek; cf. Col 3:11).
>
> So if in the Church all do not proceed by the same road, all are nonetheless called to holiness, and have obtained a faith

of equal standing in the justice of God (cf. 2 Pet 1:1). Although by the will of Christ some are appointed teachers, dispensers of the mysteries and pastors for the sake of the others, all the same there flourishes a true equality among all the faithful with respect to their worth or dignity and the activity common to all of them in building up the body of Christ. For the distinction which the Lord made between sacred ministers and the other members of his people entails also their mutual association, seeing that pastors and others of the faithful are bound to one another in common ties of relationship; the Church's pastors, following the example of the Lord, ministering to one another and the rest of the people, the people eagerly offering their co-operation to their pastors and teachers. Thus in a variety of ways all bear witness to a wonderful unity in the body of Christ; for the very diversity of graces, ministrations and works gathers the children of God into one, because 'all these things are the work of one and the same Spirit' (1 Cor 12:11).

So just as the laity, out of the goodness of God's heart, have Christ as their brother, who came, though he is the Lord of all, not to be served but to serve (Mt 20:28), so too they have as their brothers those who have been appointed to the sacred ministry and who with Christ's authority feed the family of God by teaching and sanctifying, that the new commandment of charity may be fulfilled by all. That is why Augustine says so finely: 'While I am terrified by what I am for you, I am consoled by what I am with you. For you I am a bishop, with you I am a Christian. The first name signifies an office, the second a grace; the first means danger, the second salvation'.

My only complaint about this passage (apart from the use of that overworked word 'sacred') is that it was not somehow made to govern or control the chapter on bishops and the episcopate. One tiny change from the 1963 draft is extremely significant: in the second sentence of the third paragraph the word *pro* is substituted for the word *super*. Here I have translated *pro* by 'for the sake of'; so in the earlier draft the sentence read, 'Although by the will of Christ some are appointed . . . pastors *over* the others . . .'. The note on the new text explains: '*For the sake of* others is put instead of *over* others, the better to indicate that it is a ministry of *diakonia*' (AS III, i, p. 283, note (F)).

If brotherhood and equality are the necessary antidotes for an overdose of hierarchy, sacerdotalism poisoning is best remedied by the priesthood of all the faithful. The original schema has a section devoted to this in its chapter on the laity, and explains it in the traditional way as a priesthood for the offering of spiritual sacrifices (tacitly distinguished from the 'real' sacrifice of the mass); it goes on to allow that indeed in the sacrifice of the mass the laity, as 'dedicated by baptism and confirmation to Christ the priest', may offer God the body of Christ 'through the hands of the sacrificing minister'. But then it immediately insists: 'however, in the same body they are priests properly so-called, who consecrated by the sacrament of order, appointed to act on behalf of men in relation to God (Heb 5:1), exercise the hierarchical priesthood as ministers of Christ' (AS i, iv, p. 39). Which immediately reduces the priesthood of all believers to the radically unimportant status of a metaphor, or improper mode of speech, in the traditional MP manner.

A remarkable fact is that in the commentary of this text, provided presumably by the preparatory commission which drafted it, it is acknowledged that 'In the biblical sources and in the writings of the second century, the word "priest" (*sacerdos*) is only used of Christ, of the priests of the old law, and of the people; ministers are called bishops, presbyters, presidents, etc. Nor is there any metaphysical definition of priesthood . . .' (AS i, iv, p. 44). Thus, to speak frankly, the bottom is knocked out of the statement in the text that only ordained ministers are 'priests properly so-called'. That the text remains in spite of the note is a characteristic instance of the lack of candour, the ecclesiastical dishonesty, which is a symptom of so much MP theology. That the note is there at all is, I suppose, a redeeming grace. That its contents and implications never reach the final text of *Lumen Gentium* is a case, I would say, of not co-operating with grace.

In the final document the subject is dealt with in paragraph 10 and 11 of chapter 2 on the people of God. The gaffe is avoided of saying that only the ministerial priesthood is priesthood properly so-called—as a matter of sound doctrinal fact, it is only Christ's priesthood, in the Christian context, that is a priesthood in the most proper sense. So both the priesthood of all the faithful and the ministerial priesthood are presented as participations in Christ's priesthood. The general priesthood, in paragraph 11, is shown as being exercised in the use of the sacraments, so it is given a genuine 'cultic' context, which it shares with the minis-

terial priesthood, and thus the concept of offering spiritual sacrifices (derived from 1 Pet 2:4–10) is not downgraded by being
implicitly contrasted with offering the 'real' sacrifice. I suppose
this part of *Lumen Gentium* should be read with the whole Constitution on the Liturgy in mind, and the whole work of liturgical
reform and renewal, the main thrust of which has been to emphasise the active participation of all the faithful in the Church's
worship and sacramental life, as against their merely passive
'reception of the sacraments'.

The text says (10) that 'the common priesthood of the faithful
and the ministerial or hierarchical priesthood are related to one
another, though they differ essentially and not only in degree; for
both one and the other participate, each in its own special way, in
the one priesthood of Christ'. But it says nothing more precise
about how they are related, or about the special way of each in
participating in the priesthood of Christ. The Council could
scarcely do this, in fact, because a Catholic theology of the common priesthood had been so little developed, and a theology of
the ministerial priesthood has been so overdeveloped in a wrong
direction. The Council did all it could, which was to point in the
right direction (away from hierarchical sacerdotalism), and inau-
gurate a development of Catholic theology in this sphere.

G. *Magisterium*

On this theme there is, fortunately, very little to say. We have
seen that the original draft contained a whole chapter, 7, devoted
to the Church's *magisterium*, which appears to have been designed
to push the cause of 'creeping infallibility'. This chapter, God be
praised, sank almost without trace. Some flotsam from it sur-
vived, mainly in those obsessive reiterations of the papal primacy
and infallibility to which we have already referred.

Vatican II did not of course kill the concept of *magisterium*, nor
could it possibly be expected to have done so. The concept
survives, and continues to be brandished by the MP school that
prevails in the Vatican and elsewhere. But they cannot possibly
claim that the Council underwrote the concept of *magisterium* as a
major and dominant structural element of Catholic doctrine. It
did nothing of the kind. At the beginning of this chapter I admitted, ruefully, that *Lumen Gentium* is not exactly a charter for the
ministerial collegialist or MC cause. Now at the end of it I am not
feeling quite so rueful. My opening admission is broadly true. All
the same, *Lumen Gentium*, and indeed the whole achievement of

the Council has signalled a momentous change of direction. We can picture the Council as a nervous traffic policeman, rather unsure of himself it is true, but still pointing the traffic in one definite direction. He is doing it with a tremulous finger, and frequently looking over his shoulder in another direction while he does so. Nonetheless he continues to point in that one definite direction—and it is *not* the direction in which the magisterial papalists would have us continue.

NOTES

1 To be accurate, at least one Ukrainian, Armenian and Maronite each spoke Latin.

2 *La Maison-Dieu* 165 (1986, first quarter) is entirely devoted to reflections on the local Church. Professor G. Alberigo of Bologna has a particularly stimulating, though difficult, article. Writing on the Church's response to urbanisation and industrialisation at the turn of this century, he says: 'The difficulty of adapting itself to social developments, coupled with the conviction that immobilism constitutes the best defensive weapon of the Church, has the effect of disorienting the Church. Ecclesiastical authority tries to remedy this in two main directions. First of all, it sets itself to strengthen and unify the clery by introducing a cut-and-dried distinction between "teaching Church" and "Church taught"; a distinction that radicalises the one already existing between clerics and laypeople by allotting to the first an active function, and to the latter a role that is merely passive. It is easy to see the impoverishment of the *sensus fidelium* that follows, as well as the exaltation of the identification between clergy and Church. Secondly, a new importance is attributed to the juridical organisation of the Church. A juridical "face-lift", it seems, modelled on modern civil codes, should be able to strengthen the Church; and so we come to the promulgation in 1917 of the code of canon law, which contains a unitary juridical system to govern the Catholic Church of the west in a uniform manner' (p. 66).

Later on, as he is about to conclude his review of the value attributed to the local Church from the sixteenth century up to Vatican II, he writes: ' . . . at least until the pontificate of Pius XII (1939–1958) the process of rediscovering the ecclesiological value of the local Church was going to make very slow progress . . . Account has to be taken above all of the complicated apparatus directed by the Roman curia which, by means of a network of authorisations, dispensations, reservations of judgement, approbations, maintains a system that deprives the Churches of all autonomy' (p. 70). I think I can fairly claim Professor Alberigo as an MC supporter.

3 The patriarch's French expression which I have translated 'sickly insistence' is *insistance maladive*.

9

CONCLUSION

Whether magisterial papalism will continue to control the policies and practice of the Holy See, and many of the world's bishops and episcopal conferences, in so far as they are the creation of the Holy See, fashioned in its contemporary image and likeness; or whether those who wield power in the Roman Catholic Church will begin with real courage and trust to walk manfully along the ministerial collegialist road, unmistakably indicated by Vatican II, albeit with a wavering finger, who can tell? Whichever it may be, at least we know that the Holy Spirit will be blowing where he lists, both in the Church, and in the Churches, and in the world, confounding both our darkest fears, and our illusory hopes. All I propose to do in this very brief concluding chapter is mention what in my view should be the first steps along that MC road.

I think the foundation stone of a sound MC ecclesiology is the priority of the local Church, as visible institution, over the Church universal as visible institution. But the latter is so dominant at the moment in the Catholic imagination and Catholic practice, that I think we have to start with it, and take steps to loosen it up, so to say, to enable it to make room for the local Churches to exercise their proper autonomy. So we have to begin with the centre.

The first simple but crucial step to take is to turn the triennial synod of bishops from a purely consultative body, an august talking shop as I called it, into a genuinely deliberative body,[1] that is to say into a body that with the pope can make decisions, principally legislative decisions; in other words, let it be a real synod—and with control of its own agenda.

The second, not so simple, step is to turn the Roman curia and its congregations from being an administrative, executive and legislative body into being a network of purely advisory and consultative organisations. Let the functions of the secretariats and congregations no longer be those of an administrative civil service, but of a central resource centre, collating, co-ordinating, disseminating the expertise of all the Churches in various fields. If the curia tries to govern the Church all over the world, it is bound to do it very badly—it *does* do it very badly. If it acted as a central exchange and clearing house for all the Churches, it could do it magnificently—sometimes it *does* do it magnificently.

The third step is to discontinue the curial appointment of nearly all the bishops. Bishops' conferences should be asked to work out more genuinely elective methods of electing bishops, taking into account lessons to be learnt both from history and from the practice of other Churches, both episcopal and non-episcopal Churches. There is no need for a uniform method throughout the world. There may also well be cases and circumstances where papal appointment is the best solution. And papal confirmation of elections, at least to the major or primatial sees, would still be required.

So coming to the bishops' conferences themselves, Cardinal Ratzinger's attempt to deny them all ecclesial status or authority should be firmly and definitively scotched. They should be seen as a modern revival of the ancient synodal form of Church government, and recognised as being the most proper bodies for making decisions and laws and policies best suited to the needs and circumstances of the local Churches in their areas. It should be for them to decide, for example, whether or not to ordain married men; how and on what conditions people may be dispensed from the ordained ministry.[2] It should be for them to make the final decisions about liturgy, about marriage customs, dispensations, etc., and about other points of Church discipline.

It is to be hoped that they would appreciate, not simply the value, but the necessity of admitting to their counsels representatives of the clergy, the laity and the religious (women as well as men). There is no *dogmatic* reason why synodal government should be confined to bishops, though there is a dogmatic reason why bishops should always lead it. There are historical precedents for admitting other ranks in the Church to conciliar gatherings— the mediaeval convocations, for example, not to mention general councils like that of Constance. But the initiative would have to lie with the bishops.

We saw in an earlier chapter that an unfortunate consequence of the East–West schism of 1064 was that in the West the Catholic Church came practically to be identified with the Latin Church, and the Latin Church, in virtue of some earlier precedents (the

most important of them forged) developed more and more syste-
matically into an absolute papal monarchy. What I am in fact
proposing is the 'planned dissolution' of the Latin Church into a
considerable number of distinct, autonomous 'patriarchates'—
not necessarily each with a patriarch, but each with quite as much
autonomy as the ancient Eastern patriarchates now enjoy.

Then the 'patriarchate' of the Roman see would be contracted,
let us say, to Italy—or to such other European Churches as also
consider that it would be in their best interests to belong to it.
Over all the other Churches the Church of Rome would continue
to preside in charity,[3] and its bishop, the pope, to exercise a purely
Petrine, and no longer a patriarchal authority. The cathedral
church of the Roman see is the basilica of St John Lateran. St John
the Baptist can be a model for all those who exercise authority in
the Church, especially the Petrine authority. Authority is a necessary safeguard, but the less it has to be exercised, the better. Let
the Baptist's words, Jn 3:30, always be their motto: 'he must
increase, but I must decrease'.[4]

NOTES

1 In canonical language a consultative vote is one which the superior
consulting the body in question, usually his council, does not have to
abide by; a deliberative vote is one he cannot act against. With the synod
the situation would not be quite the same; there would always, to use the
American analogy, be the papal power of veto. But to give its members a
deliberative vote would be to make them genuine partners in decision
making and legislation. As I propose it, they would be the pope's partners in all legislation for the Church universal, so that no new canons
would be made, or old ones abrogated, without their consent. The Holy
See could do worse than consult, in this regard, the Constitutions of the
Order of Preachers.
2 The dispensation of religious from their vows should be left entirely in
the hands of their superiors, acting according to their own rules. In all
cases, of course, with a right of appeal, eventually, to the Holy See.
3 Ignatius of Antioch, *Letter to the Romans*, 1.
4 What I am pleading for a substantial decrease of, is not the *plenitudo
potestatis*, the fullness of authority that is the pope's as the successor of
Peter, but the quantity of its exercise.

APPENDIX 1

Letter of Gregory the Great
to Eulogius, Bishop of Alexandria

Gregory to Eulogius, bishop of Alexandria.

Our common son, the bearer of these letters, found me sick when he brought what your holiness had written, and he has left me sick. This is why in response to the ample fountain of your beatitude I could squeeze out little more than the trickle of this short letter. But it was a gift of heaven for me on my bed of pain to receive the work of your most sweet holiness, from which I was overjoyed to learn about the doctrine of the Church of Alexandria, the conversion of heretics in the city,[1] and the harmony among the faithful; so overjoyed, in fact, that the severity of my illness was considerably alleviated. Indeed, it gives me a new thrill of joy every time I hear good news about you, though of course I do not consider it is something new in any way for you to act so perfectly in that way. That the people of the holy Church is growing, that spiritual crops are piling up in the heavenly barn, we have never doubted that this is the effect of the grace of almighty God with which you are all so wonderfully blessed. So we give thanks to almighty God, because we see fulfilled in you what is written: *Where crops are abundant, there is revealed the strength of the oxen* (Prov 14:4). After all, if a strong ox had not drawn the plough of the tongue through the soil of the heart of the hearers, so great a crop of believers would never have sprung up.

Since, however, I know that in all the good you do, you also share in the joy of others, I have something to give you in return for your grace, something not all that different to tell you: while the nation of the English, set in a remote corner[2] of the world, has continued perfidiously in the worship of stocks and stones, with the assistance of your prayers for me it has pleased God to show me I should send to that nation a monk from my monastery to preach to them. With my permission he was made a bishop by the bishops of France,[3] who helped him on his way with every assistance to the afore-said nation at the end of the world. Already news has reached us about how his work is prospering; it appears that he and his companions are sparkling with such great miracles in that nation, that they seem to imitate the powers of the apostles in the signs they perform. At Christmas last year we are told that more than 10,000 of the English were baptized by our brother and fellow bishop. I tell you all this so that you may realise what you are achieving among the people of Alexandria by speaking, and at the ends of the world by praying. Your prayers, you see, are shown to be as effective in the place where you yourself are not, as are your holy works in the place where you actually are.

On another point, I am very happy to say that your beatitude has entirely satisfied me about the heretic Eudoxius, on whose error I found nothing in the Latin language. You presented the testimony of those valiant men Basil, Gregory and Epiphanius, and so we are convinced that he must have been totally annihilated by the darts these heroes of ours hurled at him.

About these errors which, it is now confirmed, have arisen in the Church of Constantinople,[4] you have answered all my questions most learnedly, giving a judgement worthy of so great a see as yours. So we give thanks to almighty God that the tablets of the covenant are still in the ark of God. What, after all, is the mind of a high priest but the ark of the testament? Because spiritual doctrine flourishes in it, there can be no doubt that the tables of the law repose in it.

Your beatitude was also at pains to indicate that you no longer write to certain people using proud titles, which issue from the root of vanity,[5] and addressing me you add; 'As you commanded'. I beg you, please, remove this word 'command' from my hearing, because I know who I am and who you are. Your position makes you my brother, your mode of life my father. So then I did not command, but I took care to suggest what seemed to be proper. However, I find that your beatitude has been unwilling to remember what it was precisely that I drew your attention to. What I said was, that you ought not to use such a mode of address in writing to me or to anyone else. And here you are, at the head of the letter which you addressed to me, the very person who forbade it, deliberately stamping this word of pride, and calling me 'universal pope'.[6] Please, I beg your most sweet holiness not to do this to me any more. The exaggerated respect that is shown to another over and above what good manners require, simply detracts from the respect that is due to you. I, after all, do not seek to be propitiated with words, but with deeds. Nor do I regard that as an honour which I perceive to involve a loss of honour for my brethren. My honour is the honour of the universal Church. My honour is the solid vigour of my brethren. Then am I truly honoured when due honour is not denied to any one of them. You see, if your holiness calls me universal pope, you are denying that you are what you declare me to be universally— namely a pope.[7] But this must not be. Let us have done with words that inflate vanity and wound charity.

It is true, this title was offered to my predecessors by the Council of Chalcedon and by later Fathers, as your holiness knows. But none of them has ever been willing to use it, because in this world they respected the honour of all high priests,[8] in order with almighty God to preserve their own.

Finally, as I bid you a dutiful farewell, I beg you to have the goodness always to remember me in your holy prayers, so that the Lord at your intercession may release me from the entanglements of my sins—something I am unable to obtain by my own merits.

(Book 8, *Letter* 30)

NOTES

1 Following the reading in the best MSS. The text in PL reads 'over-joyed to learn about the doctrine of the heretics of the city of Alexandria, and the harmony . . .', which it is in the highest degree unlikely that Gregory wrote. A copyist's eye must have skipped a line by mistake.
2 He can never resist punning on the name 'Angles'. We have in Bede's *Ecclesiastical History of the English People* the famous story of Gregory saying 'Not Angles but angels'. Here he says 'the nation of the Angles, set in a remote angle of the world'.
3 He actually writes 'of the Germanies', the Franks (after whom France is named) being indeed a Germanic tribe.
4 Ever since the Council of Chalcedon (451) had defined the doctrine of Christ as being 'one person of the Word incarnate in two natures', whole Churches in Egypt and Syria and Armenia had broken away, and been in permanent schism; their formula was 'the one nature of the Word incarnate', and they are called Monophysites (One-nature-ites). To the

emperors this was a serious threat to the unity and stability of the empire, and for the next two centuries they tried to put forward one compromise after another to heal the breach. Gregory may possibly be referring to such a compromise; but the emperor of the time, Maurice, was attempting a policy of tolerance, so the errors the pope was thinking of may have simply been monophysitism, and its opposite, Nestorianism, raising their heads once more.

5 Cyriacus, bishop of Constantinople, had started styling himself 'ecumenical patriarch', and this strikes Gregory as the most insufferable, and dangerous, pride. So he had written protesting about it, not only to Cyriacus himself, but to the other patriarchs (he himself never uses that title), asking them not to accord this title to the bishop of Constantinople. It was above all the word 'ecumenical' he objected to—his Latin equivalent is *universalis*, 'universal'.

6 Eulogius may well have thought that Gregory objected to the bishop of Constantinople using the title because he thought it properly belonged exclusively to himself. Gregory makes it clear that his objection is to *any* bishop, including the bishop of Rome, claiming to be uniquely universal. That some sees, in particular the 'Petrine' sees of Rome, Alexandria and Antioch, have a pre-eminence and authority over others, he would not deny, nor that his own Roman see has a primacy of authority over all other Churches. He was objecting to a *style* of authority that was becoming fashionable (the Byzantine style), which saw it simply as a matter of issuing commands to subjects from a position of sacred superiority—the style adopted, in fact, by magisterial papalism.

7 Since 'pope' just means 'father', it was a title given to many of the more important bishops besides the bishop of Rome, especially to the bishop of Alexandria. Gregory's point is that if he is the universal pope, there is no room for anyone else to be called pope or father—and that again would derogate from the honour due to brethren, his fellow bishops and 'high priests'.

8 The word he uses is *sacerdotes*, usually translated simply as priests. But as here, and in most text from this period, it still refers only to bishops, it has to be translated 'high priests'.

APPENDIX 2

Written proposal of
Bishop Isaac Ghattas of Thebes (Egypt)

Bishop Ghattas submitted a proposal between the first and second sessions of Vatican II, intended as a replacement for chapters 3 and 4 of the original schema. Their place has in fact been taken by chapter 3 of *Lumen Gentium*, which therefore provides the actual text with which Bishop Ghattas' proposal should be compared.

I. The Mystery should be present in the decree, developing the eschatological aspect of the Church and an analogous concept of its membership.

II. The Council owes it to truth and justice to recognise in liberty of conscience a natural right. The Church has, furthermore, supernatural motives for affirming liberty of conscience, since its divine Founder refused to impose himself on the world by a temporal messianism.

III. The collegiality of the episcopate is the only thing that can overcome the apparent opposition between the rights of the bishops and the powers of the pope. Recognition of it is the only thing that will calm the fears of our Orthodox brethren, and the practice of it the only thing that will concretely open our doors to them. This collegiality is in any case the only episcopal *régime* adapted to the growing complexity of the modern world, both in pastoral work and in the task of evangelisation. Therefore we request that chapters 3 and 4 of the first schema should be replaced by the following text, which could form a whole section, or a subsection of the decree.

(The proposed text follows in Latin)

ON THE EPISCOPAL HIERARCHY

Chap. I: On the episcopal college

1. The episcopal college is the successor of the college of the twelve apostles. It includes all bishops, in the midst of whom stands the Roman bishop, to whom they must of necessity be linked; for Christ the Lord laid down that no authority should be exercised in the Church, except in union with the successor of Peter.

2. Transcending the diaconate and presbyterate, the episcopate is by divine law the highest grade in the sacrament of order, through which the apostolic hierarchy is perpetuated 'for the building up of the body of Christ' (Eph 4:12). Episcopal consecration is the sacrament which hands on the powers and graces of the apostles with respect to the three offices of priesthood, *magisterium* and pastoral government. And therefore the episcopate is the fullness of priesthood, and receives authority directly and immediately from Christ.

3. The episcopal college is set up as the supreme authority in the whole Church. The bishops bear together 'the solicitude for all the Churches' (2 Cor 11:28); that is to say that their Order or college both has supreme authority over the whole Church, and is empowered to define the faith of the Church with infallibility.

4. Ecumenical Councils manifest the college of bishops more openly and encourage their unity.

Chap. II: On the primacy of the Roman Pontiff

5. Although the Roman Pontiff is the equal of the other bishops in the reception of the same sacrament and in the same power of order,[1] nonetheless he has a primacy over them not only of honour but of authority and jurisdiction, to promote the unity of the Church.

6. For the blessed Peter was established by Christ the Lord, or by divine law, as the director of the universal Church, and the Roman Pontiff by the same divine law is the successor of Peter in this primacy (cf. Const. *Pastor Aeternus* ch. 2).

7. The Roman, who is also called the Supreme, Pontiff, has the supreme, full and immediate authority of jurisdiction over the

universal Church, over each and every local Church, over each and every pastor and believer (cf. *ibid.*, ch. 3).

8. 'The Roman Pontiff, when he speaks *ex cathedra*, that is, when in the performance of his office of pastor and teacher of all Christians, by his supreme Apostolic authority he defines a doctrine about faith and morals to be held by the whole Church, through the divine assistance promised to him in blessed Peter is endowed with that infallibility with which the divine Redeemer wished his Church to be equipped in the definition of doctrine about faith and morals' (*ibid.*, ch. 4); and therefore such definitions of the Roman Pontiff are irreformable, nor do they require the consent of sanction of any assembly or person. The Supreme Pontiff, however, teaches no truth in this way by virtue of private revelation. What he defines he sees, he has investigated and found, with the help of the Holy Spirit, in the mind of the Church and the teaching of the episcopate.

Chap. III: On the senate of the Church

9. The Senate of the Church, or the Sacred College, is the name of the assembly of the principal bishops, namely the patriarchs and cardinals, under the presidency of the Roman Pontiff.

10. The right of precedence before the others in the senate of the Church is enjoyed by the more venerable of the patriarchs of the Eastern Churches, in the following order: the patriarchs of Constantinople, of Alexandria, of Antioch, and of Jerusalem; the other patriarchs and cardinals according to the order of their election. In the absence of the Roman Pontiff, whoever he may appoint will preside over the senate.

11. The Senate of the Church is the Supreme Pontiff's privy council in the government of the universal Church. When it keeps him informed about the state and views of all regions of the world, it manifests the solicitude and collaboration of all the bishops for the good of the one and catholic Church. Therefore the Supreme Pontiff will summon the senate of the Church in full consistory at least every five years, and all the Fathers of the senate will assemble to review the life of the Church as a whole and in its parts. This full consistory is managed and ratified by the Supreme Pontiff.

12. On the death of the Supreme Pontiff, the senate of the Church gives him a successor according to the legitimate statutes.

Chap. IV: On the regional institutions of the episcopate

13. A bishop intervenes outside his own local Church as a member of such institutions of the hierarchy as various councils or other 'organs of co-ordination'.

14. He recognises the jurisdiction, traditional or recently acquired, of certain bishops beyond their own local Churches. These bishops are either metropolitans, or patriarchs, or autocephalous archbishops.[2]

15. An association of local Churches among the Easterners forms a patriarchate, that is a community governed by its own proper traditions and its own proper law. The patriarch supplants neither the residential bishops nor the Supreme Pontiff, but has the authority to makes provision, with the assistance of the metropolitans, for the coherence of the patriarchal community. A patriarchate, after all, is nothing but the episcopate of a particular region, unified in the person of its president or its episcopal synod, and enjoying all the powers inherited from the apostles which are not canonically barred. It is an ecclesiastical autonomy,[3] saving the primacy of the Roman Pontiff.

16. According to the canons of the Councils, the Eastern patriarchates thus hold first place in the Church after the Roman See, and their actual order is the following: Constantinople, Alexandria, Antioch, Jerusalem.

17. To meet pastoral needs, the Church can create new patriarchates or new regional autonomies, endowing them with their own proper law which will not block the prerogatives either of residential bishops or of the Supreme Pontiff.

18. The proper traditions of the ancient patriarchates do not prevent them from giving themselves a new form, to suit new states of affairs; indeed these very traditions are summoning us above all to restore unity of jurisdiction in the territories of the Eastern Churches.[4]

Chap. V: On residential bishops

19. To promote evangelisation and ecclesiastical life, each residential bishop is allotted his own territory, and he alone may exercise ordinary and proper jurisdiction over his own local Church on a permanent basis.

20. Since the bishop is by divine law the head of his own local Church, he ought to take precedence in it over everyone else,

except his own superiors in the hierarchy, namely his metropolitan, his patriarch (or archbishop or primate), and the Supreme Pontiff or his legate *a latere*.[5]

21. For the sake of unity in the Church, certain powers have been taken away from residential bishops and reserved to the Supreme Pontiff, or to the patriarch. But since the good of the universal Church cannot be based on the weakening of local Churches, this prudent limitation of authority may not lawfully degenerate into an immoderate strictness of discipline.

NOTES

1 In the traditional discussion of the sacrament of order a distinction is made in the authority which ordination confers between 'the power of order', viz. the inherent authority to celebrate the eucharist and grant absolution, and in the case of bishops to confirm and to ordain; and 'the power of jurisdiction', which used to be conceived of as not derived from the sacrament of order. Vatican II has to some extent modified this, and in principle derives the power of jurisdiction (authority to govern and teach) from episcopal ordination. But the sacrament cannot account, for example, for the peculiar papal power of jurisdiction.

2 The term 'autocephalous Church' is really more proper to the Orthodox canonical tradition, where it means a self-governing regional Church (e.g. the Orthodox Churches of Greece or Cyprus, which acknowledge in the Patriarch of Constantinople a primacy of honour, but very little jurisdiction). By 'autocephalous archbishop' Bishop Ghattas presumably means an archbishop who presides over an ecclesiastical autonomy (see next note). He is also possibly trying to 'open a door' through which Orthodox Churches like those of Cyprus and Greece could enter into communion with the Roman Church.

3 Bishop Ghattas uses 'autonomy' in a concrete sense to mean an autonomous group or society. It is not the ordinary English usage, but I have kept it in the translation.

4 The actual fact is that, although in his proposal Bishop Ghattas speaks of the patriarchates of Alexandria, Antioch and Jerusalem as if each were a single unit, there is actually more than one patriarch of each of these sees. There are the patriarchs *not* in communion with Rome: in fact in each case there is a patriarch in communion with Constantinople (an Orthodox patriarch), as well as one or more heirs of the old anti-Chalcedonian Churches, e.g. the Coptic patriarch or pope of Alexandria, and the Jacobite patriarch of Antioch. Then, at least in Antioch, there is more than one patriarch in communion with Rome. It is to this tangle of jurisdictions that he wishes to restore 'unity of jurisdiction'.

5 A rather old-fashioned term from mediaeval canonical practice. It means a legate or envoy of the pope sent for a particular occasion (sent 'from the pope's side'), as distinct from a residential nuncio or apostolic delegate. These the author does *not* wish to take precedence over the residential bishop.